Teaching with a Global Perspective

This important book answers the growing call for US institutions to internationalize, create global citizens, and better serve diverse populations. Faculty are increasingly tasked with simultaneously encouraging a more inclusive worldview, facilitating classroom environments that harness the potential of students, and advising students who may need an array of university services or speak English as an additional language. *Teaching with a Global Perspective* is an accessible, hands-on tool for faculty and instructors seeking to facilitate global classroom environments and to offer diverse students the academic, language, and interpersonal support needed for success. Rich with practical features including Classroom Strategies, Assessments, Case Studies, Discussion Questions, and suggestions for further reading in bibliographies, chapters address:

- developing a working understanding of global learning and inclusivity;
- identifying opportunities and barriers to helping students grow as global citizens;
- building confidence in teaching with a global perspective;
- facilitating courses and in-class participation that promote global and inclusive learning and communication between diverse populations;
- designing curricula, courses, assignments, and assessments that foster global and inclusive learning and support students with varied needs; and
- providing facilitative responses to students' academic work.

Teaching with a Global Perspective bridges an important divide in discussions about globalizing curricula by developing readers' content knowledge while also helping them to develop more effective global communication strategies.

Dawn Bikowski is Director of the ELIP Academic and Global Communication Program in the Department of Linguistics at Ohio University, USA.

Talinn Phillips is Associate Professor of English and Director of the Graduate Writing and Research Center at Ohio University, USA.

Teaching with a Global Perspective

Practical Strategies from Course Design to Assessment

Dawn Bikowski and Talinn Phillips

Routledge
Taylor & Francis Group

NEW YORK AND LONDON

First published 2019
by Routledge
711 Third Avenue, New York, NY 10017

and by Routledge
2 Park Square, Milton Park, Abingdon, Oxon, OX14 4RN

Routledge is an imprint of the Taylor & Francis Group, an informa business

© 2019 Taylor & Francis

The right of Dawn Bikowski and Talinn Phillips to be identified as authors of this work has been asserted by them in accordance with sections 77 and 78 of the Copyright, Designs and Patents Act 1988.

Library of Congress Cataloging-in-Publication Data
A catalog record for this title has been requested

ISBN: 978-1-138-57757-2 (hbk)
ISBN: 978-1-138-57758-9 (pbk)
ISBN: 978-1-351-26660-4 (ebk)

Typeset in Perpetua
by Out of House Publishing

To my own little global citizens, Jack and Elise.

—Talinn Phillips

To my family for all their support, my students for their
innumerable insights and stories, and my colleagues for
their patience with my questions.

—Dawn Bikowski

Contents

Foreword

A truly global university is one that is diverse and inclusive, one in which each member of the community embodies the knowledge, attitudes, and skills of a global citizen. For students, this means graduating with the foundation to be global leaders, innovators, and citizens for a sustainable world having experienced, embraced, and advanced an expectation of diversity and inclusion as a social norm. For administrators, faculty, and staff, this means committing to personal and professional behaviors that facilitate their own and student development along these lines. The imperative for a diverse, inclusive, and cooperative campus culture, however, has yet to be fully realized in our universities. Indeed, while the classroom is uniquely positioned to serve this aim, and ought to set the standard for inclusivity and be the primary driver of student development as global citizens, the challenges to doing so are substantial, and the way forward is fraught with danger. Dr. Dawn Bikowski and Dr. Talinn Phillips offer us a valuable resource by which to navigate our way as teachers with a special obligation and opportunity to move this imperative forward.

Teaching with a Global Perspective: Practical Strategies from Course Design to Assessment is deeply practical, and it is designed with care and attention to help instructors develop courses and classroom behaviors that should be standard at a global university. It offers practical, hands-on strategies from the experience of students, faculty, staff, and leadership. The authors examine numerous facets of teaching in a global classroom and they consider these from a globally aware perspective. There are valuable student voices, case studies, and strategies that guide the reader toward active work, reflection, and commitment to growth as a global citizen-teacher. Throughout, the focus remains squarely on supporting *all* students as they work through ideological struggles, miscommunications, or academic issues as they develop as global citizens.

Within these pages, Drs. Bikowski and Phillips have provided a master workshop for faculty and administrators in higher education. Adding this publication to your toolkit will guide you and your institution toward achieving the imperative for creating a truly global environment where students feel included and are inspired to develop as global citizens. While this book can be invaluable as a personal guide to one's own development as a global citizen-teacher, it would also serve as an excellent foundation for a faculty learning community or workshop series. Whether you are just beginning your journey as an educator, or you are a seasoned veteran seeking greater success in an increasingly diverse classroom, we are confident that you will find this book relevant, instructive, and inspirational.

Sincerely,
Dr. Bradley A. Cohen, Senior Vice Provost for Instructional Innovation
Dr. Lorna Jean Edmonds, Vice Provost for Global Affairs
and International Studies
Ohio University

Preface

HOW THIS BOOK CAME TO BE

We teach on a rural campus of a large US research university where international and minority students are substantially outnumbered by monolingual, white American students, many of whom have not had educational or life experiences that exposed them to diversity. A divide was growing between groups of students, with many missed opportunities to learn about and from each other. We became increasingly concerned and also committed to supporting student success by making the campus climate more welcoming and our university classrooms more accessible. We were invited to build on our expertise in working with diverse populations, language and literacy development, and global and academic communication skills in providing professional development for our faculty.

Five years ago, our dean encouraged us to expand this work by offering a new faculty learning community (FLC; a small group of faculty who study a particular issue together). Around the same time, we joined a campus-wide effort to craft a new global strategy. Our FLC branched off into additional workshops, campus surveys, and student-led focus groups, all of which emphasized the importance of holistic campus systems to foster global perspectives. Our approach needs to be one that supports not only international students in their learning experiences, but also more mainstream students as they work to develop a willingness and ability to interact with the diverse people around them (e.g., students who are African American, Native American, Latinx, Appalachian, or LGBTQ). *We all have work to do.*

We concluded our 2014 FLC by compiling a handbook for faculty. Many faculty from that learning community wrote case studies of their experiences that appear here. With support from our institution and from those learning community members, that 50-page handbook has evolved into the book you're holding. We've now used the curriculum in this book with multiple groups of faculty, incorporating their feedback each time.

OVERVIEW OF THE BOOK

Teaching with a Global Perspective: Practical Strategies from Course Design to Assessment provides an accessible, hands-on tool for faculty and administrators who seek to create a campus that is more global and inclusive in its outlook. We acknowledge that achieving this goal can be difficult (see Lilley, Barker, & Harris, 2015), and that multiple pathways are possible, but we do aim to escape the deficit model in which non-mainstream students are seen as "negative" versions of "positive" American academic culture. The book accounts for a wide range of student populations (undergraduate and graduate) through a practical, accessible approach that incorporates faculty and student voices from a variety of disciplines. It also works to quickly introduce faculty to a range of important issues in pedagogy and assessment and thus spark further study in the scholarship of teaching and learning. Although campus internationalization movements are a global phenomenon and share many similarities, we focus on the North American context and acknowledge that some challenges and potential solutions may vary elsewhere.

When we refer to "Diverse student populations" throughout the book, it includes students who may differ based on nationality, ethnicity, race, religion, social class, age, gender, sexual orientation, abilities, or education level attained by parents or family members. Faculty are increasingly tasked with simultaneously encouraging a more inclusive worldview, facilitating classroom environments that harness the potential of students, and advising students who may need an array of university services or speak English as an additional language.

Part and Chapter Organization

The book is divided into three parts with a total of eight chapters. Our goal was that each chapter could be read independently so that readers would have a quick reference point available for specific challenges. Of course, we feel that the book is most effective if read in its entirety. For those who prefer to "dip in" to individual chapters, we encourage you to begin by reading Part I in order to develop an understanding of key concepts underlying global education movements.

Part I, Foundations for Teaching with a Global Perspective, focuses on foundational concepts and on gathering contextual information important for teaching with a global perspective. Chapter 1 introduces concepts that are foundational to supporting diverse and mainstream students as they progress through higher education and develop a global perspective. Chapter 2 outlines options for institutions, faculty, and administrators to build global and inclusive learning. Finally, Chapter 3 introduces readers to the fundamentals of intercultural communication.

Part II, Curricula, Course, and Assignment Design, moves to implementation by addressing curricula, course, and assignment design. Chapter 4 introduces important principles of curricular and individual course design. Chapter 5 tackles the issue of facilitating broad participation and collaboration in class and Chapter 6 focuses on designing inclusive and accessible writing assignments.

Part III, Assessment and Feedback, concludes the book by considering how we provide feedback to students and assess programs. Chapter 7 offers principles for responding to student writing while Chapter 8 focuses on designing inclusive assessments and measuring global learning.

How to Best use this Book

Teaching with a Global Perspective can be read independently by faculty or administrators, or used as the basis for professional development, such as an FLC or workshop series. It takes a capacity-building approach in order to enable institutions to create systems in which "staff and faculty competence around diversity and inclusion is considered a core institutional value and a key indicator of success across departments and disciplines" (Mauro & Mazaris, 2016, p. 4). We've worked to support faculty who are new to course development, global education, or to pedagogy by providing an introduction to a wide range of issues and to examine them from a global perspective; thus, given our desire to make the book accessible, in-depth treatment of these issues was beyond our scope. We strongly encourage readers to use these chapters as an introduction to deeper reading.

Each chapter includes the following components:

Introduction forecasts chapter topics and provides a quick reference to learning outcomes.

Classroom and Self-Assessment allows readers to hone in on successes and opportunities for themselves and their students. Since assessing students' knowledge and values can be imprecise, readers are encouraged to gather information from a variety of students and not only the most vocal individuals. Faculty might search for examples of students making new meanings and showing development in their feelings, values, and thinking. We encourage readers to gather data at the beginning and end of a term for comparison and to use as many different approaches to data gathering to generate the broadest possible understanding. This section is intended to guide reflection, planning, and instruction. The specific information that is gathered, areas of focus, and specific impressions for criteria and levels will be best determined by faculty members.

Approaches for gathering information about your students' perspectives include:

- examining student work for mature expressions of global and inclusive understanding (e.g., through discussions, papers, and assignments);
- asking students to set and reflect on goals related to global learning and diversity within your course content;
- inviting classmates to provide peer feedback or input;
- distributing anonymous pre- and post-term questionnaires; or
- noticing students' reactions to key topics that relate to global learning.

Key Concepts provide an overview of key terms and concepts that are important for developing a global perspective. Readers more familiar with these areas may want to skim this section; readers looking for more information are encouraged to mine the *Bibliography* sections.

Classroom Strategies address key questions that faculty face in their daily work. These sections can be used as a quick reference for ideas and solutions to specific challenges.

Student Voices and *Case Studies* are vignettes that illustrate student and faculty experiences in their own words. They bring theoretical concepts to life, provide practical strategies, and encourage reflection.

The Workshop allows readers to apply the chapter to redevelop their courses, working either individually or in a group. Suggestions are practical, interdisciplinary, and guide readers step by step.

Discussion and Reflection includes questions for conversation or personal reflection that provide an opportunity to engage with topics in more depth. These questions are useful for professional development workshops or for individual analysis. Readers are encouraged to focus on the ones most relevant to their situations.

Bibliographies conclude each chapter and provide online and print-based tools that can be used to enact each chapter's principles and strategies.

 BIBLIOGRAPHY

Lilley, K., Barker, M., & Harris, N. (2015). Educating global citizens: A good 'idea' or an organisational practice? *Higher Education Research & Development*, *34*(5), 957–971.

Mauro, A., & Mazaris, A. (2016). Student recruitment and retention at the intersections: A case for capacity building. In B. Barnett & P. Felten (Eds.), *Intersectionality in action: A guide for faculty and campus leaders for creating inclusive classrooms and institutions* (pp. 3–14). Sterling, VA: Stylus.

Acknowledgments

We're grateful to the former dean of the College of Arts and Sciences at Ohio University, Robert Frank, our Senior Vice Provost for Instructional Innovation, Bradley A. Cohen, and our Vice Provost for Global Affairs and International Studies, Lorna Jean Edmonds, for the financial and professional support they provided to this project and, by extension, to our students.

We're also thankful for the many faculty who have worked with us, especially from that first, formative group who played such an important role in developing this book: Muriel Gallego, Jessica Hollis, Paula Park, Catherine Penrod, Nicole Reynolds, Linda Rice, Sherri Saines, and Sarah Wyatt.

Index of Classroom Strategies

Part I

Foundations for Teaching with a Global Perspective

Chapter 1

Preparing to Teach with a Global Perspective

 INTRODUCTION

In this chapter, we introduce foundational concepts for helping all students as they progress through higher education and develop a global perspective. The book's foundation springs from an awareness that "the university should not be distant from the tremendous problems the world faces nowadays" and should be actively engaged in both local and global spaces (Boni & Walker, 2013, p. 2), as well as evolving in order to maintain relevance and even competitiveness in an ever-changing world economy (Stein & Lambert, 2016). Thus, developing a global perspective means providing *transformative* experiences for students (Killick, 2015, p. 4) that build an ethic of inclusivity into civic engagement and social responsibility. These concepts apply to both diverse and mainstream students. Our underlying assumption is that students don't have transformative experiences simply by co-occupying space and international students don't inherently possess a global perspective. To support our students effectively, faculty must realize how their own experiences have informed teaching practices, since "our personal identities influence our professional practices" (Latino, 2016, p. 33). Thus, in this chapter, we discuss internationalization, global learning, inclusivity, global citizenry, and teaching with a global perspective.

By the end of this chapter, you should be able to:

- define key terms and discuss topics associated with a global perspective and their application to your context;
- identify approaches that allow you to teach with a global perspective;
- discuss challenges and opportunities that global learning and internationalization initiatives bring to your campus; and
- identify and discuss challenges that students from various backgrounds might face in the mainstream academic culture found in many university classes in the developed world.

CLASSROOM AND SELF-ASSESSMENT

Before reading this chapter's *Key Concepts*, begin by reflecting on your students' experiences and readiness for developing as global citizens. We also ask you to rate your own readiness to support them and teach with a global perspective. For ideas on how to assess students' knowledge and values, see the Preface. Note where you would rank your students and if their perspective seems to develop over time. This information can be used to direct your work in this chapter.

 ASSESSING YOUR STUDENTS' READINESS TO SUCCEED AS GLOBAL CITIZENS

While some courses lend themselves to helping students develop as global citizens more than others, what opportunities do students have to explore their own assumptions about diverse groups within your courses? Are there opportunities you might be missing? If students enter our courses at a different level than we expect, how does this affect course content and learning outcomes?

By the time students leave my class/department, they:

0	demonstrate very little awareness of global issues, diversity, or the role of culture and background in human behavior; have no experience with or are uncomfortable interacting with a range of people, nor do they appear to desire that interaction; are not aware of institutional academic expectations.
☆	demonstrate minimal awareness of global issues or diverse populations; show minimal awareness of or desire to learn about their own cultural biases and norms and are uncomfortable with cultural differences or people with diverse viewpoints; are minimally aware of institutional academic expectations.
☆ ☆	demonstrate awareness of how background affects behavior, yet are uncomfortable communicating in unfamiliar environments; recognize new perspectives about their own culture's rules and biases and are interested in learning more; don't only look for sameness and are comfortable with new perspectives; are moderately aware of institutional academic expectations.
☆ ☆ ☆	demonstrate awareness of global issues and interconnectedness and can explain how their own backgrounds affect their interpretations (e.g., of conflicts, triumphs, expectations, or systems of logic); seek out diverse populations and respond to biases appropriately, including shifting their own perspectives as needed; are aware of institutional academic expectations.

Example of a student at the two-star level: An undergraduate in a course discussing the global supply chain demonstrates awareness of how culture can affect human behavior, such as raising child labor as a concern in pricing and international business ethics. Less informed classmates remain silent on the issue or fail to see these connections.

Example of a student at the three-star level: An undergraduate in a Math class with an international teaching assistant (TA) is open-minded about learning from the TA and advocates for the TA in conversations with biased classmates.

Being a global citizen is thus active and should go beyond in-class discussions into real-world experiences. Students who have been provided with few opportunities to develop their own understanding of inclusivity and a global perspective will likely encounter greater difficulties in developing one during their higher education experience and will therefore require greater institutional support.

 ## ASSESSING YOUR READINESS TO TEACH WITH A GLOBAL PERSPECTIVE

As an educator, how comfortable are you working with students (e.g., during group projects, class discussions, field or lab work) to help them succeed and develop as global citizens?

In my own teaching, I:

★	am not comfortable helping students interact with people who are different from themselves or from me, or who are not aware of academic expectations. I am not sure that this is even my responsibility.
★★	want to help students succeed and interact more with diverse groups but am not sure what to do or look for. What types of behaviors indicate that students are unaware of academic expectations or are feeling left out? How do I know if they are comfortable with the complexities of encountering new perspectives, or if they are interested in learning more? How can I help, given my already limited class time?
★★★	can generally identify when students are struggling or feeling left out, or if they are having difficulties collaborating or confronting their own biases and valuing new perspectives; I can employ strategies to help students interact more positively and begin to develop as global citizens.

Example of a faculty member at the three-star level: A faculty member is sensitive to class dynamics and realizes that some students are biased against the international TA. They employ strategies to allay students' concerns and demonstrate the worth of the TA to the class while at the same time helping the TA maximize success in the classroom.

This chapter builds on these concepts and provides strategies to help faculty a) support students as they develop as global citizens, b) support struggling students who may be at risk, and c) workshop some of these concepts with colleagues.

 ## KEY CONCEPTS

Teaching with a global perspective may seem ambiguous to newcomers because it differs so widely based on context and can be implemented at the institutional, departmental, or course level. One professor might foster a global perspective by planning a trip abroad so that students can apply their disciplinary knowledge in a global context. In another class, asking students to read case studies from non-US contexts or watch an international film might be perfectly reasonable activities to foster a global perspective. Certain key concepts do apply across all situations, however, as educators seek to meet the needs of their specific students. This section provides a brief introduction to these concepts, moving from the overall topic of the internationalization of higher education initiatives to global learning, a key strategy many universities utilize to meet internationalization goals. The concept of inclusivity, which prioritizes approaches that support learning for all, is key to teaching with a global perspective. Global citizenry follows and outlines characteristics representative of this mindset. Faculty are encouraged to reflect on their own background and experiences in these areas, as well as the needs and opportunities students bring to class.

Internationalization of Higher Education

Internationalization initiatives are large and complex processes that institutions undertake in response to globalization and "on-going change across the global-local nexus" (Killick, 2015, p. 4). The effects of globalization on higher education are similar to its effects in business, the economy, or information technologies, with universities increasingly being asked to justify decisions based on market factors or on their ability to attract international students and faculty or encourage international projects or partnerships. From this increased interaction arises the concept of the global citizen.

Higher education has responded to these global trends by engaging in internationalization initiatives. Projects generally have three pillars: a) student and faculty mobility, b) internationalization of the curriculum, and c) strategic partnerships and collaborations. The term has evolved over time, particularly to emphasize the importance of opportunities being available for all, not just an elite few. De Wit, Hunter, Howard, and Egron-Polak (2015, p. 29) provide this updated definition:

> The intentional process of integrating an international, intercultural or global dimension into the purpose, functions and delivery of post-secondary education, in order to enhance the quality of education and research for all students and staff, and to make a meaningful contribution to society.

This definition highlights the goal for internationalization to lead to a better society, as well as the reality that it will likely not occur in an institution without a strategic commitment to this goal. There is an increased awareness that all courses can be internationalized (Leask & Bridge, 2013), for example through demonstrating how a discipline has been influenced by world issues. Critics have noted, however, that internationalization efforts are not always successful (see Lilley, Barker, & Harris, 2015).

International students bring many benefits to campus (e.g., diversity of perspectives; innovation; increased revenue, research, and patent applications), but campuses also experience extra services, cost, and workload with an increased international student population. Teaching with a global perspective entails providing domestic students with strategies to create a welcoming campus and international students with the services and support they need. In addition to academic language support, international students may have unique needs related to their awareness of academic and social expectations in the learning environment. Many students, regardless of their country of origin, benefit from coursework or services that support them as they develop their skills in academic literacy and communication.

The following *Student Voice* of a graduate student from Japan illustrates the classroom repercussions and consequences that occur when students do not feel a sense of belonging.

STUDENT VOICE: WHAT I LOOK LIKE WHEN I FEEL LEFT OUT

"Hand cuffed and a towel in my mouth." That is how I feel when I am in a classroom with an instructor and classmates who do not seem to care what I am feeling. Going to a class which makes me feel this way is challenging not only academically, but also challenging to even bring myself to the classroom. During my stay in the United States, I heard numbers of people say "If you have a problem, you have to stand up for yourself" or "Speak your mind." I agree it is an important skill set to succeed in this society; however, I also would like classmates and my instructor to understand that these are values in American culture. In some cultures, people are taught how to endure hardships without speaking up. It takes time to change these customs. When I cannot follow expectations from the culture in the US, people assume they know why I'm being quiet—that I'm not being responsible for my learning, and not participating in class. In reality, that is an interpretation from just one side. The stories of our side are usually misheard and ignored.

I hope sharing my experience will lead to opportunities for instructors and students to communicate to make inclusive classrooms. After all, an inclusive classroom is created by not only the instructor, but also students in the class. In the following, I offer four points you could look for in your classroom, along with why I was acting in a certain way.

When I felt that the instructor did not care regarding my learning, I did not make eye contact with the teacher or classmates. I was frustrated and also ashamed that I could not follow the class conversation. I could have asked for explanations; however, if my confusion stems from the frequent use of phrases or notions rooted in American culture, I will have to keep asking questions every class, which will annoy professors and classmates. If students are not making eye contact even during discussions, that may mean they need assistance from the instructor or classmates.

Another cue is not speaking up. It could simply mean that students are not accustomed to share their opinions in public, given that some education systems do not teach this skill. However, if I do not feel I am welcomed to speak, I will remain silent. Sometimes not only classmates, but also instructors, do not respond to what I share in class. A teacher not responding to what an international student shares sends a message to the class that the student can be treated that way. How your domestic students treat international students is a reflection of how you interact with international students. International students may be silent in your class not because they do not understand, but rather because they feel not welcomed to share.

When you see a student not give any verbal and nonverbal reactions to a question, that is also an SOS signal. It could be a response to what you asked, or related to interactions between students. When I feel my thoughts or experiences do not matter for a teacher or classmates, I do not give any reactions in the class. If they do not care, why should I risk showing what I am thinking or feeling? What I share could lead me to another problem, for example, "She does not have critical thinking skills" or "It does not work that way in the US." For students to be able to express their thoughts and feelings, the environment has to be safe. If students do not give any reactions to a teacher or other classmates, that can show how safe they feel in the classroom.

My story does not represent all international students. Every international student is different, just like domestic students. Yet, because of cultural or linguistic differences, our behaviors or words are too often misinterpreted. Before you decide on what you think a student is like, please communicate with the student with a non-judgmental attitude. Sometimes students' actions are not from disrespect, but rather represent struggles in the class. It is a very simple thing; however, realizing that there is a story you do not know will open an opportunity for conversation.

Miwa Tokunaga
Graduate Student from Japan

Miwa Tokunaga's poignant comments make clear for faculty just why it is so important to help our students develop a global perspective. It often requires extra attention to look for behaviors that indicate a student is feeling left out in class or within your institution; thus, one key strategy many universities pursue in internationalizing their campus and fostering a sense of belonging is engaging all students in global learning.

Global Learning

Global learning is one path to internationalization and takes on different forms depending on the educational setting and priorities (Schattle, 2008); in general, however, it is planned instruction that encourages students to become informed and open-minded as they are mindful of diversity, work toward understanding how their actions affect others, and approach problem-solving from a collaborative and equitable standpoint (American Association of Colleges & Universities, AAC&U Global Learning VALUE Rubric[1]). Landorf and Doscher (2015) provide an action-based definition of global learning as "the process of diverse people collaboratively analyzing and addressing complex problems that transcend borders" (p. 24). The AAC&U has divided this complex topic in their Global Learning

VALUE Rubric into six dimensions: global self-awareness, perspective taking, cultural diversity, personal and social responsibility, global systems, and knowledge application. Global learning thus provides opportunities for students to cultivate an open attitude while further developing their knowledge and skills in this area. It necessitates diverse students interacting in meaningful ways (e.g., through project- or team-based learning on relevant topics, or through education abroad) and sufficient support for all students on campus (e.g., awareness of academic expectations, campus support resources, faculty support during activities involving intercultural communication). Foundational principles essential to global learning include contextualizing knowledge, reflecting on content and learning, being able to shift perspectives, and feeling a sense of responsibility for diverse others (Kahn & Agnew, 2017).

Global learning benefits individuals as well as society. It can foster greater learning (de Wit et al., 2015), contribute to national security and cultural diversity, lead to workplace preparedness, and facilitate economic competitiveness (Scott, 2005). However, challenges arise as campuses strive to further develop the global outlook of their students and to retain diverse populations. For instance, costs associated with global learning programs (e.g., education abroad) leave many students unable to take advantage of these experiences. Increases in the number of students from diverse backgrounds can lead to tensions or conflict (e.g., a lack of communication or ineffective communication, misunderstandings, stereotypes, resentment, or hate speech). Students' disinterest of other viewpoints or inability (or unwillingness) to understand various World English accents (e.g., English as spoken in India) can pose a major threat to classroom dynamics. Increased campus diversity can also lead to faculty and staff needing to spend more time meeting individual student needs and also learning about or creating on-campus support systems. Given that skills associated with global learning are increasingly prioritized, however, campuses will continue to seek to engage in this area.

While internationalization initiatives and global learning imply a more inclusive outlook at home and abroad, practitioners often emphasize the global and international components. The concept of inclusivity and educating all students is, however, crucial in global learning and one that merits time and attention.

Inclusivity

The concept of inclusivity has evolved from providing discrete populations with discrete services (e.g., accessibility office, LGBTQ office) to a more integrated approach that fosters a sense of belonging on campus for diverse students. Inclusive education thus refers to an education that embraces and fosters the well-being and "effective, sustained participation" of all learners (Barton & Armstrong, 2008, p. 6), with the mindset that opportunities are lost if anyone is excluded in classroom learning. This approach also acknowledges that identities change over time and that students often view themselves as belonging to many different groups simultaneously (Mauro & Mazaris, 2016). Therefore, campuses might benefit from taking an intersectional approach (Barnett & Felten, 2016) and increase collaboration, such as between the international student office and the multicultural office. Advocates call for faculty from across campus and various disciplines to be involved in some capacity in creating more inclusive classrooms (Latino, 2016). The following *Student Voice* of an undergraduate minority student illustrates the powerful role that faculty can play in helping students feel a sense of belonging.

STUDENT VOICE: HOW MY PROFESSORS EMBODY INCLUSIVITY IN THE CLASSROOM

During my time at Ohio University I have had several professors who made efforts to include their students of color in their classroom teaching through material, discussions, and assignments. As a journalist, it is particularly important that we serve as constant students to the cultures around us, both domestic and international. My teachers have made sure to embody this along the way.

Specifically, very early in the semester I have been in classes that attempt to break down our hidden biases, pointing out that we all have them. Spring semester of my junior year, I remember being the only black person in my Public Relations Writing course and suddenly feeling uncomfortable because I realized, surprisingly, this had been the first time I'd been in this situation at Ohio University. We did an exercise where we had to stand up if we identified with a sentence; I was dreading the "I am African-American," sentence. Sure enough, it was read and I stood up. I felt the blood rush to my cheeks and thought to myself, "why would she do this?" but after my getting past the shallow feeling of awkwardness, I realized the bigger purpose. I stood up for so many more things, joining many classmates, than just that one sentence. Although I may have been alone in my skin tone, I was not alone in my interests, life experiences, and passion for journalism.

Through intentional efforts to identify the differences in our classrooms, my professors have made me feel included. I have never once been asked for my opinion by a professor on a topic just because of my skin tone. Students are a different story, as this happens quite often in the classroom. But, I have felt comfortable enough in the majority of my classes to speak up when being a black woman has given me the experience to chime in with a valuable opinion. It is in fact those uncomfortable times that push us to use differences such as skin tone to educate those around us. I am appreciative of the efforts my professors have made to create an inclusive classroom where this is possible.

Hannah Britton
Anticipated BS in Journalism
Ohio University

Hannah Britton's story is particularly compelling in that it illustrates how faculty can work toward inclusive classrooms. Often, it is our intentional efforts that will have the most impact on students' experiences and sense of belonging in our classrooms. This classroom environment plays a large role in supporting students as they become global citizens.

Global Citizenry

The term "global citizen" is frequently used but infrequently fully defined or mutually understood (Lilley et al., 2015). However, it typically entails three key components: global competence, social responsibility, and civic engagement (Morais & Ogden, 2011). Another potentially ambiguous term, "global competence," is "a state of readiness to engage and interact with others from their own perspective" (Rhinesmith, 1996, as cited in Jean Francois, 2015, p. 40). Global citizenry is thus active in seeking to open one's own mind and in working toward the good of others. While this term has received criticism for prioritizing a Western-nation perspective (Schattle, 2009) and can seem unattainable, it offers a certain amount of shared understanding among practitioners, promotes a growth mindset (Lilley et al., 2015), and is widely used. It also implicitly entails the concepts involved in inclusivity, such as belonging, participation by all, and respect (Schattle, 2008). Therefore, for the purposes of this book, the term *global citizen* will be used, with the understanding that inclusivity is embedded in this concept and that the term indicates a continuum and ongoing opportunities for development.

The key knowledge, attitudes, and skills of a global citizen fall into three main areas. The *knowledge* global citizens need includes an awareness of one's own situation in life and how it is similar or different to others' experiences as well as the role of culture and background in human behavior. It also entails an awareness of others, including a general understanding of global politics and interdependence (Schattle, 2008). *Attitudes* of a global citizen include feeling secure in one's identities and learning spaces and being comfortable within unsettling environments while maintaining tolerance and curiosity about others

(Killick, 2015); a willingness to work through awkward, difficult, or unclear communication, a "language pain tolerance" (Lilley et al., 2015, p. 962); a sense of "moral connectedness" with all of humanity (Lilley et al., 2015, p. 963); and a sense of empathy, respect, responsibility, and motivation to interact with and advocate for diverse populations (Schattle, 2008). *Skills* include the ability to carefully and openly listen to differing viewpoints; the ability to communicate with others from different languages or backgrounds; the ability to work through miscommunication or to negotiate conflict; and the ability to think critically and ethically (Lilley et al., 2015).

The following *Student Voice* outlines an undergraduate student's path to developing as a global citizen.

STUDENT VOICE: GAINING A GLOBAL PERSPECTIVE

I grew up in a pretty typical community. We shared a collective world perspective by which ideas were measured and digested. Sundays were reserved for church, sports teams were the line between friend and foe, and potatoes were served with every dinner. Folks in my community found comfort in our common perspective, which meant broadening that perspective was far from typical. It wasn't that seeing the world differently was a negative value, it was just that habit and routine were easier to come by. No one really knew any differently.

The first time I ventured beyond my typical community was high school. It wasn't too far from home, but it was far enough that I met people from different religious backgrounds and had teachers with unfamiliar accents. My Spanish teacher injected my worldview with energy that no one else in my community had done previously. She shared stories of growing up in Mexico and traveling to places I'd never heard of like Xochimilco. I wanted more.

I was the first generation in my family to go to college. Having my curiosity piqued in high school, I made it my mission to surround myself with opportunities to broaden my worldview. I picked International Studies as my major because of the study abroad requirement. I also joined a program called the Global Leadership Center because it required students to have two overseas experiences. University became a great place to explore the limits of my worldview—what I valued as true and "typical" back home could suddenly be reassessed. I surrounded myself with professors and students who shared stories and experiences from their lives, allowing me to imagine a new way of life. It was a magical time—the world as I knew it still had so much to discover.

I had a lot of natural curiosity for expanding my boundaries, but it was my professors along the way who gave dimension to the dreams and possibilities of seeing the world differently. I had an anthropology professor who lived among chimpanzees in Africa, an international relations professor who grew up in Soviet-era Belarus, and a business professor who lived many years abroad in different countries. These professors instilled in me excitement and curiosity about the world's varying perspectives, and through sharing their experiences they showed me that even I could gain a global perspective.

Gaining a global perspective takes a village outlook. Looking back, I wonder what my life would be like if certain professors hadn't impressed upon me the value of broadening one's worldview. Perhaps I wouldn't have aspired to earn a Fulbright scholarship to Malaysia and live in an Islamic community. Perhaps I wouldn't have ever dared to join the Peace Corps and stay in El Salvador for five years working on community development projects. Perhaps I wouldn't have ever gone to graduate school in Japan through a Rotary World Peace Fellowship because I wouldn't have believed in the value of an international educational perspective. My professors could've just taught me math, science, and English, but by relating the material to a more connected global experience, they taught me so much more. Their belief in challenging one's way of thinking and questioning what we think of as "typical" changed my life, setting me off on a path of curiosity which I'm still on today.

Zachary Garinger
Ohio University alumnus (BA Global Studies),
Rotary World Peace Fellow, and Fulbright awardee

One of the most powerful elements of students' stories is realizing the great influence that education can have on someone's life. Zachary Garinger's story highlights the importance of cumulative experiences and of role models, some of whom likely had no idea that their own lives were so impactful to others. Classrooms that prioritize curiosity and a willingness to engage with diversity provide the catalyst many students need in order to develop as global citizens.

Teaching with a Global Perspective

This book's focus is *teaching with a global perspective*, or understanding and meeting the needs of all students in increasingly diverse classrooms. Teaching with a global perspective means using the concepts above to work toward internationalization initiatives, for example through internationalizing the curriculum or seeking to improve the quality of education for all. It also addresses the concerns of global learning, aiming to increase students' curiosity in others and further develop their critical thinking and problem-solving skills. When we teach with a global perspective, we strive to create an inclusive campus for all students, increasing participation from diverse groups and also facilitating the development of students as global citizens within the confines and opportunities of each discipline. An instructor's awareness of issues and realities related to global learning affects teaching in many ways—for example in choosing course learning objectives, choosing materials or case studies, forming in-class discussion questions and facilitation, setting up and moderating group projects, and writing assessments. Our own knowledge of the world, attitudes regarding diversity, and skills in communicating with diverse others affect our students' learning experiences.

For more traditional, domestic university students, teaching with a global perspective often entails helping them develop a global citizen mindset. In addition to global citizenry skills, diverse students may need extra support with academic literacy or language skills. All students want to feel that they belong

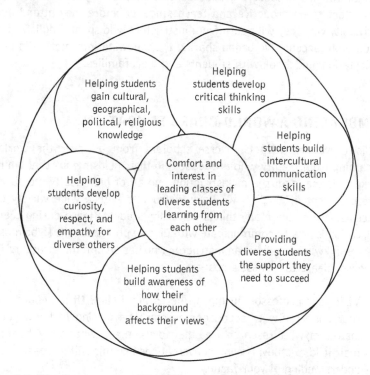

Figure 1.1 The Components of Teaching with a Global Perspective

in our classes. Being aware of potential student needs is the first step in teaching with a global perspective. For, while no faculty member feels fully capable to meet the needs of all their students, we can all choose to take part in the journey toward more inclusive, global, teaching practices.

The key components of teaching with a global perspective are represented in Figure 1.1.

The following *Case Study* illustrates how campus administrators can help students develop a global perspective and embrace global education—in this case, with students who view different English accents as a barrier to their success.

CASE STUDY: "HELP! MY PROFESSOR DOESN'T SPEAK ENGLISH"

One of the most popular complaints made to our walk-in advising center at the beginning of each semester is "I can't understand my professor!" While each academic advisor has developed strategies to work through this concern with students, we also recognized that it was important to be proactive and teach students before they attend our university why they will learn from instructors who speak English with a different accent. We began sharing the following information in our orientation guidebook with students and their families.

EMBRACING A WORLD-CLASS EDUCATION

Ohio University attracts diverse scholars from all over the world. Learning from faculty who are leaders in their fields means that while English is the language of instruction and all of our faculty members are proficient in English, we have instructors with a wide variety of accents. One of the many things university students learn during their education is how to communicate with diverse professionals. To be most successful when you have an instructor who has an unfamiliar accent in English, please take these steps:

1. **Visit your professor during his/her office hours.** Office hours are your opportunity to spend one-on-one time getting to know your instructor, what research area they focus on, and what drew them to their field of study. Having conversations like this will increase your understanding of your faculty.

2. **Listen carefully in class.** Communication is a two-way street, and while speaking English requires effort for someone who grew up speaking a different language, native speakers also need to put forth effort to understand those who are trying so hard to communicate well. Sit up front, take notes, and follow the book or any materials during the lecture.

3. **Ask questions in class when you don't understand.** Engaging with faculty members in the discussion about a topic will help them see what you have understood and what they need to spend more time explaining. This will increase your understanding of the material.

We tell students that we hope they will value and appreciate the world-class education they receive, and that while we may be in a small town, we offer access to scholars from a wide variety of countries who contribute a wealth of knowledge and culture to their education.

Jenny Klein
Assistant Dean for Success and Persistence
Ohio University

This *Case Study* shows how important framing and explanations are as we support students learning to learn from others. As campus professionals, we do value the education and exposure that international faculty and TAs bring to campus, but sometimes we may forget that students will not always make these connections on their own.

 ## CLASSROOM STRATEGIES

Common questions about teaching with a global perspective follow, ranging from basic needs for teaching with this mindset to creating the right type of environment for global learning.

"What do I need to understand in order to teach with a global perspective?"

Some things to keep in mind as you approach the often sensitive topics of diversity, culture, identities, and stereotypes:

- *Know yourself.* Spend some time reflecting on your background to gain insight into your teaching decisions, since our teaching styles are based on our own worldviews and identities. How well are you able to "appreciate, engage, and practice empathy" across all types of students (Mauro & Mazaris, 2016, p. 6)? Do you have any biases or stereotypes that might be an obstacle to teaching with a global perspective? Investigate your own biases online at Harvard's Project Implicit (https://implicit.harvard.edu/implicit/).

- *Know your students.* Spend some time learning about the backgrounds and identities of your students to help guide classroom decisions about content or participation style. Try exit slips, where students answer or pose questions, reflect on course content, or connect content to their own lives. Or have students complete polls or surveys anonymously. Learn about campus resources and help students find the support they need. If possible, consider inviting or even requiring students to attend your office hours in order to build rapport, start conversations, and instill confidence.
- *Monitor questions and assumptions.* Consider how your range of students can contribute when you are writing your discussion questions or activities. Also, students may be excited to make friends outside of their comfort zones. Or they may not. While some students enjoy being asked where they are from or asked to share experiences from their culture or background with the class, others feel the question can automatically tag them as "other."
- *Look for teachable moments.* Differences in communication styles and personality types offer intercultural communication and learning opportunities, not just barriers. Don't be afraid of potential miscommunication; instead, plan for it and be prepared with strategies when it occurs.

"How can I create an environment that is conducive to helping students develop as global citizens?"

Building a global perspective begins with faculty prioritizing an equitable and inclusive classroom. Strategies to try include:

1. Help Students Build Interest and Curiosity in Others
- *Articulate the benefits of a global understanding.* For students motivated by grades, require behaviors consistent with a global perspective or assignments that foster interaction with diverse people in order to achieve high grades. Create in-class experiences that encourage (or require) students to interact across racial, national, and class backgrounds. For students focused on their careers, provide examples of how a global

understanding or intercultural communication skills will contribute to their future success.

- *Encourage students' interest in people and your course topic beyond their comfort zones.* Find out what interests students and work toward connecting that interest to specific areas in your discipline. Try having diverse students, guest faculty, or professionals lead discussions (online or in person) in order for students to hear about diverse perspectives from a safe and trusted source. Use simulation games (e.g., Spent at playspent.org, about surviving homelessness and poverty) to build understanding and empathy. Remind them that being out of their comfort zones can be unsettling and is a temporary stage in the process.
- *Encourage students to ask themselves if they are being diverse in their choices.* They can look at who they reach out to for friendships, who they talk to in class, what types of events they attend or movies they watch, or even the food they are willing to try.

2. Develop a Sense of Belonging Where Students Feel Safe in Taking Risks and Making Positive Contributions

A safe learning space is particularly important for those who are more likely to feel excluded; it necessitates building in activities that foster security in your students' knowledge, behavior, and emotions (Killick, 2015). Inclusive classrooms also increase the likelihood of students seeking help. For example:

- *Share your own global perspective with students.* Acknowledge that you are affected by your background and that you look forward to students educating you on their experiences.
- *Be inclusive in your speech and in who you call on in class.* Students can be invited to notice classroom dynamics in your own and other classes, noticing if students from diverse backgrounds appear to feel comfortable. Look for and build upon opportunities in which students from non-dominant campus groups can be the experts or at least on a similar footing.
- *Build in a feedback mechanism for students' feelings of belonging.* This can be with names or anonymous. For example, students can be asked, "Are there any points of view that we might be overlooking?"

3. Help Students Identify and Question Damaging Stereotypes

Be aware of possible problematic or offensive generalizations that have been socially normalized and therefore may seem appropriate to state in class. Comments about undocumented residents or crime, for example, might offend or harm some student populations but seem socially acceptable to others. Helping students identify damaging stereotypes can occur at many levels, both in the classroom and also in individual conversations. Examples include:

- *Hold students accountable for their words.* Ask students why they are responding in a more hostile or dismissive manner, allowing them to reflect on the cause of their feelings. Address any potentially biased or dismissive behavior and help students realize the damaging impact that stereotypes have on their view of the world, for example with interpreting news or even casual campus conversations.
- *Include inclusive content.* Include course content (particularly with multimedia) that shows multiple viewpoints to give students the opportunity to think from others' perspectives.
- *Help students see other perspectives.* Ask students to turn a situation around or pretend they are in an opposite position and then question how their opinions might change. For example, you might create a series of course-appropriate problem-solving scenarios similar to the one in Workshop 3.2, Intervening to Build Successful Intercultural Communication.

4. Initiate Conversations between Students

- *Help different student populations mix.* Guide groups that exhibit minimal or no communication by helping them develop topics to discuss or to work through misunderstandings. Ask questions to prompt students back into discussion or prepare them by leading discussions on how miscommunications might occur; offer strategies for working through confusion.
- *Support students as they develop their "International English" speaking abilities.* For native English-speaking students, this means that they communicate in a way that maximizes comprehensibility, for example minimal use of idioms or slang, choosing less complicated grammatical structures, and speaking at a steady rate. For multilingual students, "International English" means helping them to be comfortable with the English abilities they have and being willing to take risks in communication, as opposed to allowing concerns over accuracy to impede their willingness to communicate.
- *Encourage students to be excited about being welcoming hosts to your international population.* Identify diverse student populations who your students can welcome with picnics, social and/or cultural events, or informal discussions on succeeding in your campus environment.

5. Give Students the Language to Discuss Their Concerns and Feelings

As students realize that the words they choose reveal their worldview and beliefs, they often learn to make more respectful choices. We discuss intercultural communication in more depth in Chapter 3, but below are some initial strategies to try:

- *Ask students to notice and refrain from using language that may offend others.* Examples are culturally based phrases or labels, or general comments that prioritize their group over others. Statements such as "In this/my country, we expect…" are often inflammatory and hurtful.
- *Help students respond to potentially divisive remarks.* Offer them language options that demonstrate respect, such as how to respectfully disagree or challenge potential stereotypes.

 THE WORKSHOP

1.1 Increasing Your Global Perspective through Professional Development

Refer back to this chapter's Self-Assessment, the section on Global Citizenry, and the Components of Teaching with a Global Perspective as shown in Figure 1.1. Then try completing these sentences as you create your own individualized, behavior-based plan, grounded in your discipline and the courses you teach. This workshop focuses on the knowledge, skills, and attitudes you bring to teaching, in addition to areas for development.

I could be more globally focused in my *knowledge* by…

I could be more globally focused in my *skills* by…

I could be more globally focused in my *attitudes* by...

Reflect on your answers in light of this chapter. What three or four goals do you have for the upcoming semester or year as you further develop your ability to teach with a global perspective? What behaviors or evidence can you collect to help you determine whether you've met your goals? Take a look at the bibliography to identify resources to help you achieve your goals.

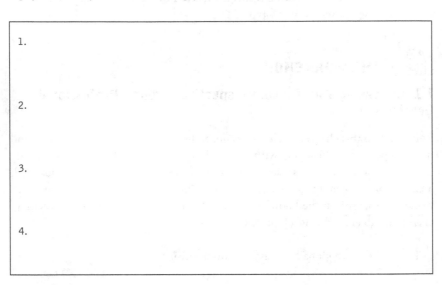

1.

2.

3.

4.

1.2 Identifying Obstacles to a Global Perspective

Refer back to this chapter's Classroom Assessment and identify obstacles to your students developing as global citizens. Be as specific as possible and have an eye toward resolution. For example, some students are hesitant to engage in conversations with classmates of different backgrounds. We often identify language as a barrier to interaction, but what specific difficulties do you see? Is it just that an international student has an accent, or is it also that your domestic students aren't comfortable or lack strategies for speaking with someone who speaks a different variety of English? Or, perhaps different groups of domestic students aren't comfortable working together. What is holding them back?

Identify potential obstacles in the appropriate areas:

- Language (e.g., English, academic writing or speaking skills):

- Self-confidence level or insecurities about their own identity:

- Communication skills or social skills:

- Past learning experiences and assessments:

- Opportunities for interaction inside and outside the classroom:

- Motivations and rewards for all types of students to interact:

- Other:

Next, consider any minor (or not-so-small) changes you can make or approaches you can try in order to reduce some of these obstacles in your context and create supportive, curiosity-driven, environments. Reflect on data you can collect to help determine if the changes allowed you to meet your goals.

Changes to consider:

1.

2.

3.

4.

5.

1.3 Understanding and Appreciating Your Students' Backgrounds

Review the *Student Voices* and *Case Study* in this chapter. Consider your students as you answer the following questions:

- What are their backgrounds (e.g., race/ethnicity, educational level, countries of origin, socioeconomic level, etc.)?

- What benefits do diverse student populations bring to your classes?

- What are some of your students' key needs, and are they being met?

- Do you notice any behaviors that lead you to believe that some students may be feeling left out in class or in your institution?

Note any potential areas you may want to focus on in your course design or class environment here:

 DISCUSSION AND REFLECTION

1. What benefits appeal to you about global and inclusive learning? What benefits are likely to appeal to your students?
2. How are internationalization and diversity initiatives impacting your campus? What are some of the challenges as well as opportunities facing faculty, staff, and students?
3. Reflect on your own personal story and multiple identities—how do they influence your attitudes, worldview, or behaviors in your teaching? What transformative educational experiences have you had and how can they guide your interactions with students who may be facing similar questions or situations?
4. In what ways does your discipline allow you to focus not only on key content areas, but to at least touch on issues related to helping students develop as global citizens in their knowledge, attitudes, and/or skills?
5. Examine the AAC&U Global Learning VALUE Rubric (www.aacu.org/valuc/rubrics/global learning) and the descriptions for each of the levels of proficiency. Do you see ways you can apply this as you contribute to students' development as global citizens?

NOTE

1 The Global Learning VALUE Rubric (www.aacu.org/value/rubrics/global-learning) divides each dimension into four levels of proficiency and can be used to guide the design and implementation of both curricular and co-curricular learning experiences and allow student growth to be assessed over time. It is one of 16 VALUE rubrics (www.aacu.org/value-rubrics), i.e., critical thinking, intercultural knowledge and

competence, and lifelong learning. Samples of global learning definitions from various institutions can be found in their Shared Futures: Global and Social Responsibility initiative (www.aacu.org/global-learning/definitions).

 BIBLIOGRAPHY

American Council on Education's Center for Internationalization and Global Engagement (www. acenet.edu/news-room/Pages/Center-for-Internationalization-and-Global-Engagement.aspx). Supports institutions as they develop internationalization strategies with its Internationalization Toolkit.

Association of International Education Administrators (www.aieaworld.org/). Brings international education leaders together with an annual conference and programs and awards.

Barnett, B., & Felten, P. (2016). Introduction. In B. Barnett & P. Felten (Eds.), *Intersectionality in action: A guide for faculty and campus leaders for creating inclusive classrooms and institutions* (pp. xiii–xix). Sterling, VA: Stylus Publishing.

Barton, L., & Armstrong, F. (2008). Policy, experience and change and the challenge of inclusive education: The case of England. In L. Barton & F. Armstrong (Eds.), *Policy, experience and change: Cross cultural reflections on inclusive education* (pp. 5–18). London, UK: Springer.

Boni, A., & Walker, M. (2013). Introduction: Human development, capabilities and universities of the twenty-first century. In A. Boni & M. Walker (Eds.), *Human development and capabilities: Re-imagining the university of the twenty-first century* (pp. 1–12). London, UK: Routledge.

Center for International Higher Education (www.bc.edu/bc-web/schools/lsoe/sites/cihe. html). Flagship publication is *International Higher Education* (https://ejournals. bc.edu/ojs/index.php/ihe); Worldwide Higher Education Inventory (www. bc.edu/bc-web/schools/lsoe/sites/cihe/IHE1/worldwide-higher-education-inventory.html) provides information about main centers for graduate-level programs and research on higher education internationally.

De Wit, H., Hunter, F., Howard, L., & Egron-Polak, E. (2015). *The internationalisation of higher education*. European Parliament. Retrieved from www.europarl.europa. eu/RegData/etudes/STUD/2015/540370/IPOL_STU%282015%29540370_EN.pdf

Institute of International Education (www.iie.org). International non-profit organization with publications, best practices resources, and services related to building international programs. Their Open Doors report provides detailed information on students and scholars studying abroad and about international students and scholars in the United States.

Jean Francois, E. (2015). *Building global education with a local perspective: An introduction to glocal higher education*. New York, NY: Palgrave Macmillan.

Kahn, H., & Agnew, M. (2017). Global learning through difference: Considerations for teaching, learning, and the internationalization of higher education. *Journal of Studies in International Education*, *21*(1), 52–64.

Killick, D. (2015). *Developing the global student: Higher education in an era of globalization.* London, UK: Routledge.

Landorf, H., & Doscher, S. (2015). Defining global learning at Florida International University. *Diversity & Democracy*, *18*(3), 24–25.

Latino, N. (2016). Leadership at the intersection: A developmental framework for inclusive leaders. In B. Barnett & P. Felten (Eds.), *Intersectionality in action: A guide for faculty and campus leaders for creating inclusive classrooms and institutions* (pp. 25–35). Sterling, VA: Stylus Publishing.

Leask, B., & Bridge, C. (2013). Comparing internationalisation of the curriculum in action across disciplines: Theoretical and practical perspectives. *Compare*, *43*(1), 79–101.

Lilley, K., Barker, M., & Harris, N. (2015). Educating global citizens: A good 'idea' or an organisational practice? *Higher Education Research & Development*, *34*(5), 957–971.

Mauro, A., & Mazaris, A. (2016). Student recruitment and retention at the intersections: A case for capacity building. In B. Barnett & P. Felten (Eds.), *Intersectionality in action: A guide for faculty and campus leaders for creating inclusive classrooms and institutions* (pp. 3–14). Sterling, VA: Stylus Publishing.

Morais, D., & Ogden, A. (2011). Initial development and validation of the global citizenship scale. *Journal of Studies in International Education*, *15*(5), 445–466.

Schattle, H. (2008). *The practices of global citizenship*. Lanham, MD: Rowman & Littlefield.

Schattle, H. (2009). Global citizenship in theory and practice. In R. Lewin (Ed.), *The handbook of practice and research in study abroad: Higher education and the quest for global citizenship* (pp. 3–20). New York, NY: Routledge.

Scott, P. (2005). The opportunities and threats of globalization. In G. Jones, P. McCarney, & M. Skolnik (Eds.), *Creating knowledge, strengthening nations: The changing role of higher education* (pp. 42–55). Toronto, Canada: University of Toronto Press.

Stein, J., & Lambert, L. (2016). Leaders, governing bodies, and advisory boards. In B. Barnett & P. Felten (Eds.), *Intersectionality in action: A guide for faculty and campus leaders for creating inclusive classrooms and institutions* (pp. 36–47). Sterling, VA: Stylus Publishing.

Pathways to Global and Inclusive Learning

 INTRODUCTION

This chapter discusses programs and models that institutions can use as they build a global and inclusive campus, ranging from large-scale institutional initiatives to classroom-based projects. The focus is on the end goal of students learning and developing as global citizens, with many possible paths to that goal. Campuses will be most successful when they involve administrators, faculty, staff, and students from across diverse groups in order to build a multi-faceted, context-specific model. While institutions increasingly include "a global perspective" in their mission statements, few provide robust interdisciplinary opportunities for global learning to occur. Students are not always aware of the initiatives or able to articulate how their experiences have led to increased global learning or intercultural communication skills (Whitehead, 2017). Furthermore, global learning appears to occur less within the sciences (Musil, 2006), even though each discipline has a role to play in meeting the goals of these initiatives (Leask, 2015). Given the fragmented reality of global education in the United States:

> colleges and universities need to sharpen their aims and develop more coherent global education curricular programs ... and convey in clear language to students what they are expected to achieve in terms of global learning by the time they graduate.
>
> (Musil, 2006, p. 3)

Faculty and staff play a key role in the success of these initiatives; in fact, Nair and Henning (2017) point out that often what initiates curricular and campus change is "an organic set of ideas" that arise from the faculty (p. 8). Building on foundational concepts from Chapter 1, this chapter provides practical strategies from the institutional to the classroom level and provides an overview of potential resources for faculty and students.

By the end of this chapter, you should be able to:

- identify programs and models that are often utilized to support global and inclusive learning on your campus; and
- identify activities to help students develop as global citizens in your classroom.

 ## CLASSROOM AND SELF-ASSESSMENT

Before reading the following section on pathways to global learning, take a moment to reflect on your awareness of institutional initiatives and resources to encourage global learning and student support. For ideas on how to assess students' knowledge and values, see the Preface.

 ## ASSESSING YOUR AWARENESS OF INSTITUTIONAL INITIATIVES OR RESOURCES TO ENCOURAGE GLOBAL LEARNING AND OFFER STUDENT SUPPORT

As an educator, how much do you know about resources available on your campus to help students develop as global citizens and/or to succeed in their coursework?

In my own teaching, I:

★	am not sure what resources are available to help me teach with a more global perspective. I am also unaware of the resources available to students to help them develop as global citizens or to succeed in coursework if they need additional academic support.
★★	am aware of a few resources to help me teach with a more global perspective, but I have utilized them only minimally. I know about some academic support for students but would have only minimal advice on developing a global perspective.
★★★	am aware of and have used several institutional resources to help me teach with a more global perspective. I know about and regularly refer students to resources for support academically and to develop as global citizens.

Example of a faculty member at the three-star level: A faculty member in a natural sciences course creates a system that identifies at-risk students early on in the semester by utilizing low-stakes assignments. Students with scores below the threshold are asked to meet with the professor to identify barriers to success in the class and possible support services on campus. The professor and university support office(s) maintain open communication and future assessments and assignments are monitored, with adjustments to support being offered as needed.

 ## KEY CONCEPTS

Creating a class climate of inclusivity that encourages global citizen values requires involvement from across the campus. Comprehensive campus involvement implies there is an appropriate administrative structure and staffing; a globally focused curriculum, co-curriculum, and learning outcomes; faculty policies and practices that prioritize global education; and meaningful collaboration and partnerships (American Council on Education, 2017). Yet, as Reimers (2014) laments, despite many initiatives, universities are still not preparing students to be global citizens. Initiatives are most successful and sustainable when they are connected to established coursework or faculty processes and procedures such as release time or tenure and promotion (Nair & Henning, 2017). The manifestation of global learning on each campus will differ based on context and resources. This chapter specifically addresses opportunities that highlight global learning; many high-impact educational practices (Kuh, 2008, e.g., learning communities, undergraduate research, writing-intensive courses) can also be planned with a global component in mind. While other types of offshore global learning exist, for example transnational or offshore education (when a university has an overseas campus), the focus here is on international initiatives that take place within national boundaries.

Given that students enter our classes at various levels of preparedness to experience transformative learning (see Merriam, Cafarella, & Baumgartner, 2007), some may find themselves in the stage of critical reflection, while others will be ready for more extensive personal development. Our initiatives and coursework will be most useful when they meet students where they are and help them move toward their goals.

Much of the work in helping students develop as global citizens comes down to three steps: a) helping create or foster a sense of curiosity and interest in diverse groups, b) giving students opportunities to learn more and communicate with diverse individuals, and c) supporting all students as they work through any ideological struggles, miscommunications, or academic needs.

Some of the ways that these concepts can be integrated more formally into the student experience can be found below, moving from campus-wide to classroom-based initiatives and concluding with a Framework for Structuring Global Learning. Students can be involved in their own development by creating and reflecting on goals as they learn to be more inclusive in their thinking. See the Bibliography for more information.

Internationalization of the Curriculum and Co-Curriculum

Many institutions begin global learning projects with efforts to internationalize their curriculum. Internationalizing a curriculum is a comprehensive task that involves "the incorporation of international, intercultural, and/or global dimensions into the content of the curriculum as well as the learning outcomes, assessment tasks, teaching methods and support services of a program of study" (Leask, 2015, p. 9). The process requires many steps. After collaboratively identifying institutional goals related to global learning, committees identify courses where the goals can be met (e.g., general education courses), and departments work to realize those goals in their own coursework. Garnering support from across campus is essential. Efforts to internationalize the curriculum may or may not lead to the actual development of a global perspective in students, and simply adding objectives to existing courses or creating new globally focused course requirements for students is not sufficient. Other types of learning experiences, preferably where students interact with diverse peers and are supported by faculty, are often needed. Institutions are encouraged to go beyond the internationalization of their curriculum as they assist students in their growth, such as internationalizing the co-curriculum (learning experiences, activities, or programs offered by the institution that complement the curriculum). Extracurricular activities (activities, clubs, or programs that aren't directly related to the curriculum) can also contribute to students' global learning through increased opportunities for interaction.

Workshop Series or Certificate Programs

Offering students a certificate or course credit for completing a series of courses, workshops, extracurricular activities, or exchange experiences is one way to motivate them to engage in topics that will allow them to develop as global citizens. These vary based on campus opportunities, goals, and leadership. Florida International University, for example, offers the Excellence in Global Learning Medallion honor for students who complete at least four courses with a Global Learning focus, complete a significant number of co-curricular activities related to Global Learning, complete a capstone project, and submit a personal reflection (Landorf & Doscher, 2015). Or, courses can be certified according to stated criteria, such as through the Global Citizens Project at the University of South Florida. On a smaller scale, departments can offer their own version of awards or certificates for students who complete coursework, projects, or extracurricular activities that focus in this area.

Support Offices, Advising, and Mentoring

Offices with mission-specific goals to support diverse and potentially marginalized populations can be found on most campuses, for example a multicultural office, international student office, LGBTQ office, etc. Additional academic support is often available in academic centers, advising centers, accessibility offices, or tutoring or writing centers. Unfortunately, these services are not always created to foster collaboration across offices (Barnett & Felten, 2016), necessitating institutional will in order to raise communication and awareness. Increased partnerships can lead to larger projects, such as the workshops that Kalamazoo College offers which increase capacity-building among faculty and staff and include topics such as eliminating racism (see Barnett & Felten, 2016, p. 53). These offices can provide vital leadership and expertise as a campus works to become more inclusive and inviting.

Variations in expectations and needs for mentoring and advising diverse students can require specialized skills and experience. While some students may appreciate a more relational style to mentoring (e.g., self-disclosure), others may be looking for technical conversations and less support on an emotional or social level (Johnson, 2016). The mentor–mentee relationship can be affected by the amount of information or identity (e.g., sexual orientation) that a mentee feels comfortable sharing, yet potentially marginalized students may face additional pressures or concerns due to discrimination or inaccurate assumptions in teaching or advising. Promoting an open environment and using inclusive language is thus key in mentoring diverse students; also helpful is becoming aware of needs that specific groups may have, developing self-awareness regarding stereotypes and communication style, and becoming aware of various strategies to demonstrate attentive listening (Johnson, 2016). All faculty and staff can help diverse students find the support they need and assist them as they build a healthy campus network.

The following *Case Study* outlines some needs faced by diverse populations on campus, as well as services and mentoring approaches that may benefit them.

CASE STUDY: MENTORING MINORITY STUDENTS

I reached the most definitive moment of my adult life when I received a scholarship to study in the United States. It was not only the allure of further education that marked this juncture, but also the opportunity to live in and experience the culture of the most powerful and diverse country in the world. As a teenager, I was perpetually intrigued by the grandeur of the American dream, the richness of the US constitution, the complexity of its political structure and the contradictions of its social mores.

While this opened new worlds for me, it was also a time for reflection. By the time I had completed my first degree, I began questioning how some educators are able to connect with all students while others struggle to create inclusive classroom spaces. As a result of my experiences, I developed an educational philosophy to provide a unique opportunity for students to learn, live, and grow in a dynamic and diverse community. Like many, I believe education should offer students more than just knowledge; it is a vital component of life experience. Yet in reality, our educational systems sometimes paralyze students instead of preparing them to be critical thinkers who can be refreshing catalysts for positive change—in essence, citizens who can function seamlessly in a global context.

As director of our university's Office of Diversity and Inclusion and Multicultural Programs, I've developed the following three goals in order to help my students embrace the cultural, economic, and political environments in which they live. First, I want my students to develop self-discipline, establish meaningful relationships, and become responsible members of the community. Second, I want my students to value individuality, in persons and in thought, and third, I want my students to think critically. I also recognize the importance of trust between students and educators in building successful relationships. Engaging with situations that students face daily allows me, and all faculty, to go beyond the theoretical, and look toward the practical.

I have been successful in the classroom because of how I operationalize these goals. I develop authentic relationships with students. This involves engaging them outside the classroom, such as attending functions hosted by the groups and organizations that they are part of. This also involves utilizing individuals and examples from their communities (when possible) to develop shared understanding. I also provide honest and constructive feedback (I am not afraid to hurt their feelings) and demonstrate how important this is for engaging in the real world. Since I want my students to see me as more than just their "teacher," I educate myself about the (targeted) resources that are available on campus so that I can assist them with challenges outside the classroom. For example, when a group of African American females was having a hard time making connections on campus I invited them to my office and asked them about their interests. They were interested in finding African American female mentors. I reached out to the Women's Center and learned about several mentoring programs on campus.

Most importantly, I've learned it's important that I model the behavior that I'm encouraging my students to follow. I also recognize that while I have expertise in some areas of multiculturalism, I am not an expert in all areas, so sometimes I seek out other experts. I also seek out and join professional development opportunities to improve teaching and communication skills. The way I see it, we're all life-long learners.

Dr. Winsome M. Chunnu
Strategic Director for Diversity and Inclusion
and Multicultural Programs and Initiatives
Ohio University

Winsome Chunnu's *Case Study* illustrates the power of personal relationships and taking a few minutes to get to know students who may need our guidance. As she points out, showing our students that we are all working toward the goals of a global perspective and lifelong learning is key.

Education Abroad and/or Language Learning Experiences

Education abroad experiences can be transformative for students. At one time, institutions viewed study abroad and/or language learning experiences as being the key to students developing as global citizens. Over time, however, it has become clear that more avenues are needed, not only due to the prohibitive expenses of travel but also due to challenges that education abroad can present (e.g., choosing not to interact with people from the local culture; increases, not decreases, in stereotypes and feelings of superiority; difficulties in connecting education abroad experiences back to their on-campus learning). While institutions continue to prioritize education abroad experiences, and in fact are developing more rigorous assessment measures, most universities have expanded into other types of more economical and feasible measures to help students engage in global learning. Often, campus communities fail to fully utilize the passion and knowledge that students bring back with them from their international experiences. We are likely surrounded by students who have completed an education abroad project and may be appropriate as resources for our courses (e.g., guest speakers, intercultural communication coaches, group facilitators, peer mentors). These students can share not only their language- or culture-related experiences, but perhaps more importantly, intercultural communication skills that they developed. Education abroad experiences are most useful for students when they are integrated into mainstream higher education (see Lewin, 2009).

Research into education abroad shows that the greatest student learning results from programs with a clear academic focus and those that articulate learning outcomes. Students also demonstrate greater learning when there are opportunities to become more globally aware and engage in field-based learning. Students should be advised to consider not only countries of interest to visit, but also academic, professional, and civic goals they have for the experience, so that these learning opportunities truly provide a clear added value beyond what they can attain with on-campus learning (Tarrant, Rubin, & Stoner, 2014).

Internationalization at Home Experiences

A movement that began at the end of the 20th century (see Wächter, 2003), Internationalization at Home (IaH) is a flexible concept that refers to experiences that allow students to develop a global perspective and intercultural communication skills while in their own countries. Acknowledging that not all students can study abroad, Beelen and Jones (2015) offer an inclusive and comprehensive definition as "the purposeful integration of international and intercultural dimensions into the formal and informal curriculum for all students within domestic learning environments" (p. 69). These experiences involve embedding "international and intercultural perspectives into local educational settings" (Turner & Robson, 2008, p. 15). Taking advantage of cultural opportunities within an institution's region is a strength of IaH. This might mean structuring opportunities for students to welcome and engage with diverse students in your institution. Other possibilities include developing community or area field trips that draw on the diversity of the area, or longer stay-away options that allow students to interact with unique communities. For example, US students studying Spanish might travel to the American southwest to study southwest culture and Spanish language. Technology has greatly expanded the types of IaH projects now available, as we discuss below.

Online Intercultural Exchange Projects

Online Intercultural Exchange (OIE) refers to technologically mediated, collaborative projects between groups of students located in different regions or countries; it allows for content knowledge exchange and also the development of intercultural awareness and/or language skills between the different groups (Lewis & O'Dowd, 2016). OIE projects can be combined with study abroad or IaH programs as well. The State University of New York's Collaborative Online International Learning Network, or COIL, is a model that has become increasingly popular, as it provides a structure and support for team-taught courses with a shared syllabus that emphasizes collaborative and experiential learning (Rubin, 2016). Project-based OIE allows groups to engage in research and recommendations for a real-world client, usually one that is relevant to both groups in some way. Problem-based learning OIE projects ask groups to discuss case studies and issues on complex cultural matters, allowing for an understanding of other perspectives and types of contributions. A hallmark for these projects is the relationships that students often make, increasing the possibility for growing curiosity and interest in other perspectives and cultures. Intercultural communication skills are developed somewhat naturally as students work toward a shared goal. These projects do require serious involvement from the instructor, however, in terms of project design (Müller-Hartmann & Kurek, 2016), ongoing student support and monitoring (Helm, 2016), and assessment (Hauck & MacKinnon, 2016). Yet the success of these projects emphasizes that the domain of international projects in coursework has expanded, as they are now often housed outside of formal language classrooms.

The following *Case Study* illustrates how a COIL project has been used to increase Appalachian students' cultural awareness and intercultural communication skills.

CASE STUDY: COLLABORATIVE ONLINE PROJECTS TO INCREASE DOMESTIC STUDENTS' GLOBAL UNDERSTANDING

When I started my career as an instructor thirty years ago, I was excited to demonstrate real cultural competence to my Appalachian and first-generation students—I wanted to share my culture with them and try to understand theirs as well. I wanted them to have opportunities to study abroad or interact with people different from themselves, knowing that students who travel outside of their country are able to learn more about the world and develop intercultural understanding. However, for the majority of my students, education abroad is not feasible.

That's why I was excited to have been selected by my university to participate in a COIL project. After receiving training on structuring a COIL class and building international partners, I decided to make my Gender course into a COIL course with a university in Honduras. Out of that class, I decided to make a four-week unit a COIL project for this first attempt. My partner and I chose the topic of cultural differences in gender-appropriate behavior as the focus of our unit. Prior to conducting our online discussion activity, we prepared students for the topic through assigned readings and group discussion. Then we created a Facebook group and placed students in small groups, with students from both countries sharing a short video of themselves that included a self-introduction and a few words on gender behaviors in their countries. After students got to know each other, we asked each group to gather information on gender values in their own cultures as well as compose questions for their international partners on the values they have in their countries. My Appalachian students solicited information from their Honduran peers, and the Honduran students asked questions of my students. The groups took time to code and identify several gender differences and write them up into a group report. Each student also wrote a brief reflection paper about their experience.

A COIL project does take extra preparation and the results of the project are a bit unknown, but that is one of its strengths. For my students, this activity was a useful supplement to class lectures and the research we had been discussing. The students also had first-hand information from members of a different culture, an experience that they may not otherwise engage in. The flexibility of the exercise is another of its strengths. The information and examples can be tailored to the specific students' experiences, and discussions tend to be different with different student groups. Overall, students reported a positive learning experience, as well as a high level of enjoyment both getting to know members of another culture and learning about how others view the world. They felt more dedicated to learn about others not only through what they read on social media, but through personal experiences and communication. They learned about their own and 3–4 different cultures by interacting with students of different racial, ethnic, religious, and socioeconomic backgrounds, as well as different sexual orientations.

Devito (2003) noted that communication, not genes, transmits culture. As international and intercultural education continues to gain the attention of educators, we can't leave our less advantaged students behind. Through programs such as COIL we can provide opportunities for all students to develop the crucial skills of intercultural competence and communication, taking me back to the reason I began teaching these topics thirty years ago.

Dr. Sheida Shirvani
Professor of Communication Studies
Ohio University-Zanesville

This example provides one type of online intercultural exchange project and model, showcasing the steps faculty can undertake to make these experiences successful for students. A further benefit of OIE projects is that they can vary in length and in assignments.

Experiential or Global Service-Learning Projects

Experiential and service learning are part of a larger movement of place-based education, which is "anytime, anywhere learning that leverages the power of place [...] to personalize learning" (Getting Smart). In the context of global learning, place-based learning models can bridge the local to the wider world. Experiential learning is one example and implies active learning through experience coupled with reflection (Kolb, 2015). Often working in groups, students can work for or with partners from inside (e.g., student support offices, libraries, student clubs or groups, etc.) or outside (e.g., local businesses or non-profit organizations) the university. Students are given the opportunity to apply course concepts to their lives or in their communities. Projects can be large- or small-scale, but clear guidelines and assessments are crucial, as are opportunities for students to process their experiences. Educators can utilize tools such as the reflection map (Eyler, 2002), which guides students through reflections on their own, with classmates, and with the community at large. Sample projects for helping students develop as global citizens include working with the university to further integrate marginalized groups into campus life or working with a small business to boost sales with international students. Another option is structuring opportunities for domestic students to be good hosts to international students or faculty. Projects are most successful if the students, usually working in groups, and the partner both benefit from the information that is found or shared. Final reports or presentations can be included as appropriate.

Service learning is experiential learning that shares a commitment to "a vision of education that synthesizes both action and reflection" (O'Grady, 2000, p. xv) and involves students working within a community, usually on a socially conscious project. A specialization within service learning is global service learning, "a community-driven service experience that employs structured, critically reflective practice to better understand common human dignity; self; culture; positionality; socio-economic, political, and environmental issues; power relations; and social responsibility, all in global contexts" (Hartman & Kiely, 2014, p. 60). Students, for example, can work with a local environmental organization to increase diversity in community involvement. They could also be connected with local refugee or immigrant communities for projects or dialogue. Departments can also include global learning outcomes in their existing service-learning experiences so that students can apply global competencies in their fields. International service learning can be even more transformative for students, offering increased gains in intercultural competence, understanding of global issues, and an expanded worldview (Pless, Maak, & Stahl, 2011). In this way, various initiatives can overlap, such as an education abroad experience that includes service learning.

In-class Faculty Initiatives

Institutions are increasingly looking to faculty across the entire campus to teach with a global perspective. Faculty may turn to some of the options discussed above (e.g., experiential learning), they may add a global dimension to their courses, or they may seek to expand their students' intercultural communication skills through group projects or case-study analyses. Disciplines that don't typically assume a role in developing students' global perspectives can analyze the needs their graduates have in this area. Accounting students, for example, need to be able to "think, communicate, and act beyond their home jurisdiction" (Leask, 2015, p. 33), while public relations students can be encouraged to reflect on the field as "a cultural activity influenced by social, political, and cultural contexts and actively involved in the construction of meaning" instead of an area in management (Leask, 2015, p. 39). Faculty in the natural sciences can bring non-Western ideas into the classroom or use intercultural or international case studies (Agnew, 2012). Technology can be utilized to build awareness of students' own cultures as well as others, for peer-to-peer learning, or to build intercultural communication skills. Social media tools or other low-cost options can provide ease of use with high interest for global learning. In-class polling software or automatic response systems can be used to facilitate discussions and information sharing; blogs or discussion forums can encourage less vocal students to share their views. How faculty in all fields structure and conduct their classes undoubtedly impacts students' development as global citizens. Institutions that offer several options and opportunities to all students will be the ones that excel in this area, given that no one course or faculty member can provide sufficient experiences to transform a student into a global citizen.

The following *Case Study* illustrates the importance of a campus internationalization strategy and articulates how that strategy can be built collaboratively through faculty, administrators, and staff.

CASE STUDY: BUILDING A GLOBALIZATION STRATEGY

Universities strive to produce graduates who will serve as global leaders, innovators, and citizens for a sustainable world. It is the job of the university leadership to support faculty in this very challenging endeavor. At Ohio University, working as a newly appointed Vice Provost of Global Affairs and International Studies with the Associate Director and our team, we were asked by the President to support the university in building its global strategy. We embarked on a multi-step process that continues today to guide our decision-making and investments in globalization.

The first step was to ensure that the global strategy was aligned with the university vision statement:

Ohio University will be the nation's best transformative learning community where students realize their promise, faculty advance knowledge, staff achieve excellence, and alumni become global leaders.

We next examined global trends and pressing issues in higher education while collecting benchmarking data on our global past and present. We asked: "What can aid our university to be nimble and inclusive as we strive to achieve strategic goals for globalization in an ever-changing world?" And, "What institutional strengths can we call on as we intentionalize global learning?" Or "What barriers will we need to address?"

Our third step was thus identifying stakeholders and holding a series of global strategy meetings. We asked participants to collectively shape the story that we wanted to tell about our institution to ourselves internally, to our current and prospective students, to our alumni and partners, and to the outside world. Out of these meetings and discussions came the ideas and concepts that we used to refine our framework.

The chart in Figure 2.1 below shows the most current framework that was ultimately used throughout the process and continues to do so as we advance our strategic interests.

Meetings across departments, colleges, and campuses, and among partners led to our vast array of activities and programs finding a home in one of the four outcomes or in the supporting priorities. The process of collaboratively and iteratively building this framework took a year, but it was a year well spent. We were then able to share the framework widely through various channels (e.g., our web presence and ongoing face-to-face engagement) and identify key investments.

Identifying priorities is never easy; in our case, we arrived at a set of activities with investment requests for mainstreaming globalization over the next five years: 1. recruiting and supporting global students and alumni with a focus on the international community; 2. achieving excellence in a global academic mission with a focus on supporting faculty and staff recruitment and development; and 3. creating a supportive environment for an informed global community with a focus on internal and external relationship management and coordination that increases global visibility and performance. Of equal significance was the emergence of "*diversity, inclusion, and cooperation*" as the defining

Figure 2.1 Ohio University's Framework for Strategic Globalization

agenda for the university's global mission of "leading globally for good; preparing global leaders."

Ohio University's strategy for globalization for 2016 to 2020 was identified and presented to the Board of Trustees Academic Committee in Fall 2016. Although our globalization framework will remain constant, our strategic priorities and its activities must continue to evolve along with the challenges facing higher education and our world.

A well-integrated strategic framework with a transparent and accessible process of information sharing and storytelling makes innumerable impacts. Most important is its nimbleness to help the university adapt to an ever-changing world and produce the plans and activities to achieve its vision. Many new strategic initiatives have emerged since this process began which support one or more of the three strategic priorities. The imperative to globalize the curriculum was identified as a strategic area for investment and development, which led to a series of "globalizing the curriculum" workshops and the publication of this book! It led to our Student Senate creating its first ever "Global

Vision" with a "Bill of Rights" that embraces globalization. Of significance is that all of us—administrators, department chairs, faculty, students, and alumni—are now able to see the depth and breadth of our global activities and, more importantly, the impact that they are making. And this framework has provided a means of benchmarking current practices to identify metrics to measure progress. It is enabling the university to align its resources and infrastructure to facilitate an ongoing process of engagement and implementation of the strategy. It is telling our story.

The university now has a common tool and language to continue to discuss the strategic priorities of globalization and opportunities for collaboration that will foster cooperation, synergy and even greater impact. The rewards are self-evident—a road map and commitment to graduating citizens and leaders who are *confident, competent, connected, cooperative,* and *compassionate.* It is this skill set and enthusiasm that will enable them to enrich livelihoods and contribute to the sustainability of our "world within the universe" and the infinite possibilities ahead of us!

Dr. Lorna Jean Edmonds and Dr. Ji-Yeung Jang
Vice Provost and Associate Director
Office of Global Affairs and International Studies
Ohio University

This *Case Study* illustrates the importance of collaboration across campus in forming a globalization strategy. Finding a place for everyone to fit in is crucial to success for a strategy, so that it exists not only on the page, but as a living document in the institution.

Putting It Together: Structuring Global Learning

The Framework for Structuring Global Learning (see Figure 2.2 below) illustrates the interaction of the global learning components outlined above. As the figure demonstrates, faculty play a crucial role as they choose which elements of global citizenry (knowledge, skills, attitudes) to focus on in their teaching and as they shape and also are guided by a shared campus vision. Staff interactions help determine the degree to which students feel that a campus is inclusive and infused with a global perspective. The base of the pyramid illustrates the components of institutional commitment, without which a global campus cannot be achieved. Professional development opportunities (e.g., workshops or learning

Figure 2.2 Framework for Structuring Global Learning

communities, lectures, collaborative teaching opportunities, faculty education abroad experiences, certificates) can help ensure that faculty and staff communication, teaching, advising, and support are reinforcing institutional goals and priorities. Professional development and goal setting can include the creation of a map of campus-wide services, offices, coursework, etc., that are available to support all students on campus. Faculty and staff can use this tool to identify areas of potential collaboration, as well as areas that may require greater intentionality in order to ensure that global learning is being addressed (e.g., see New York University Abu Dhabi in Barnett & Felten, 2016, p. 8). Considerable time and resources are required for comprehensive campus-wide planning, and teaching with a global perspective can be messy and ambiguous, yet opportunities for learning beyond the classroom are often very powerful and can be affordable options to build on classroom experiences.

This framework outlines the components that contribute to a campus that prioritizes global and inclusive learning. The crucial topic of assessing student learning, both at the institutional as well as classroom level, is covered in Chapter 8.

CLASSROOM STRATEGIES

The questions below focus on ways to utilize existing resources or classroom experiences to help students develop as global citizens.

"What initiatives might be available on my campus to help students develop as global citizens?"

Many institutions have workshops, discussion series, or collaborative initiatives that may lend themselves to topics related to global citizenry and inclusive education. Try looking for these options:

1. Difficult Dialogue Series

Many universities have a Difficult Dialogue discussion series. Questions related to identity, culture, or background can be included in this series. Even questions such as "Where are you from?" can affect students in different ways based on their identities and past experiences. While some students appreciate being asked about their origins and view the question as an opening to conversation, others resent the question and feel they are being consistently reminded of their outsider status. They may prefer questions such as "Where did you grow up or attend high school?" or "Tell me about yourself" which embrace a more universal experience. These kinds of topics can be explored in a Difficult Dialogues series.

2. Forums with University Student Groups

Your Student Senate or other campus organizations may be interested in holding a forum where complex issues can be discussed among peers in a safe environment. Questions can include thinking forward such as, "If you were dropped on a college campus that had a global perspective, what would that look like?" or "Do you have a friend or know a classmate with a global perspective? What characteristics do they possess?" When difficult topics arise, have a plan to facilitate smoother communication and increased learning (see Chapter 3).

3. Student Workshops or Courses

Workshops can be voluntary for students or required within a course. One model is hosting a 3-hour experiential workshop on themes with global appeal (e.g., various conflicts, child labor or human trafficking, sustainability in tourism). Participants work in groups and are assigned roles germane to the workshop theme, ranging from key players in leadership positions to those with minimal institutional or societal power. The groups then work together to identify competing agendas, understand viewpoints and priorities, and strategize for a common solution. In this way, students are supported as they explore skills related to perspective taking, applying knowledge, and exploring the ethics of social responsibility. In workshops, students can also be encouraged to identify ways they can be good hosts to international students on campus. Learning outcomes can be developed from the Global Learning VALUE Rubric offered by the Association of American Colleges & Universities (www.aacu.org/value/rubrics/global-learning). The experience can culminate with students submitting a final product such as a reflection essay or presentation. For faculty who don't teach within the humanities or social sciences, course content can be linked to student workshops held on campus. Reaching out to workshop organizers with ideas for science students, for example, is one way to offer interdisciplinarity to the series. Students who have completed an education abroad experience can be invited to classes to speak about other cultures or their intercultural communication experiences. Courses can also be created that prepare students to become global citizens by focusing on how to communicate with people of different backgrounds or perspectives.

"How can I create more experiential learning opportunities for my students?"

Consider beginning on a smaller scale before undertaking more complicated projects. Try working through these steps:

1. Examine your course content for opportunities for service learning or experiential learning. Is there overlap between your content and organizations that are affiliated with your university or community? For example, do you teach plant biology and have access to a community gardening space? If so, can you incorporate into your garden not only the foods most often associated with your locale but also those that may be rooted in different regions or cultures? Does this biology project allow the opportunity to bring in a guest speaker about the role of food in our families or culture?

2. Once you have identified opportunities for service or experiential learning, you can seek potential collaborative partners. Options include field trips, joint projects, or guest speakers. Key to the success of these projects is ensuring that both your class and the project partner can benefit from the experience.

3. Identify specific, mutually beneficial project goals that will meet your course requirements and be interesting to your student population. Work

on a project timeline with your partner and establish clear guidelines and grading rubrics for students.

4. Once the project is underway, be sure to monitor student engagement in the topic as well as their ability to connect it to their lives and field. Allowing opportunities for students to experience other perspectives is vital.

 ## THE WORKSHOP

2.1 Identifying Campus Resources

Given the siloed nature of many campuses, it can be difficult to keep up with the resources available to faculty and students. Start by taking inventory of campus support. Talk with colleagues, your center for teaching, or your Dean of Students in order to identify the offices or supports available on your campus, such as:

- academic support courses
- disability and accessibility services
- Gender and Women's Studies Department
- help and advising centers
- international student services
- LGBTQ services
- multicultural office
- religious organizations
- writing centers
- Women's Center

Identify campus offices you are interested in learning more about and how they might help you develop a deeper understanding and/or support specific student populations:

Office #1

Support offered or relevance to your teaching situation:

Office #2

Support offered or relevance to your teaching situation:

Invite colleagues or campus professionals to review and give feedback on your syllabi, assignments, online materials, or policies. Consider asking the following:

- What is the message of inclusivity and openness that my materials send to students? Are there opportunities to make my materials more inviting to various campus communities?

- Are there other faculty or staff on campus who work on similar projects and in what ways might they provide feedback or possibilities for collaboration?

2.2 Contributing to Global Learning Initiatives in Your Institution

Look over the pathways to global learning, as well as the Framework for Structuring Global Learning (Figure 2.2), and the *Classroom Strategies* above. In which areas can you contribute to global learning on your campus or in your course?

- Faculty or Staff Approach

- Comprehensive Campus-wide Planning

- Learning beyond the Classroom

Sharing your ideas with a colleague or chair/supervisor often opens up new ideas or potentials for collaboration, in addition to providing a level of commitment and accountability.

DISCUSSION AND REFLECTION

1. What history does your institution have related to international students and diverse populations (e.g., amount of diversity on campus, student backgrounds, initiatives). How might past experiences be impacting your students' potential for global learning today?
2. What is your institutional mission and core values, and to what degree do they include concepts related to global learning? Can you find examples that may guide you in course planning or teaching?
3. What pathways to global learning might you or your department consider implementing?
4. Did you have international experiences as a student? How did they impact your global perspective? Looking back, do you think your institution provided sufficient support and opportunities for you to get the maximum benefits from those experiences?
5. What are some strategies that have worked for students who are learning to build a global perspective and embrace diversity?

 BIBLIOGRAPHY

Agnew, M. (2012). Strategic planning: An examination of the role of disciplines in sustaining internationalization of the university. *Journal of Studies in International Education*, *17*(2), 183–202.

American Council on Education. (2017). CIGE Model for Comprehensive Internationalization. Washington, DC: American Council on Education. Available at: www.acenet.edu/news-room/Pages/CIGE-Model-for-Comprehensive-Internationalization.aspx

Barnett, B., & Felten, P. (2016). Introduction. In B. Barnett & P. Felten (Eds.), *Intersectionality in action: A guide for faculty and campus leaders for creating inclusive classrooms and institutions* (pp. xiii–xix). Sterling, VA: Stylus Publishing.

Beelen, J., & Jones, E. (2015). Redefining internationalization at home. In A. Curaj, L. Matei, R. Pricopie, J. Salmi, & P. Scott (Eds.), *The European higher education area: Between critical reflections and future policies* (pp. 67–80). Dordrecht, The Netherlands: Springer.

Devito, J. (2003). *Human communication: The basic course* (9th ed.). Boston, MA: Allyn and Bacon.

Difficult Dialogues National Resource Center (www.difficultdialoguesuaa.org/national_movement). Offers information on dialogue strategies, campus initiatives, handbooks, and a resource center.

Eyler, J. (2002). Reflection: Linking service and learning—Linking students and communities. *Journal of Social Issues*, *58*(3), 517–34.

Getting Smart. (n.d.). *What is place-based education and why does it matter?* eduInnovation and Teton Science Schools. Available at: www.gettingsmart.com/

Global Citizens Project at the University of South Florida (www.usf.edu/gcp/). For faculty and students, offers the Global Perspective Inventory, the Global Citizen Award program, or the Global Citizens course certification process.

Hartman, E., & Kiely, R. (2014). Pushing boundaries: Introduction to the global service-learning special section. *Michigan Journal of Community Service Learning, 21*(1), 55–63.

Hauck, M., & MacKinnon, T. (2016). A new approach to assessing online intercultural exchange: Soft certification of participant engagement. In R. O'Dowd & T. Lewis (Eds.), *Online intercultural exchange: Policy, pedagogy, practice* (pp. 209–231). New York, NY: Routledge.

Helm, F. (2016). Facilitated dialogue in online intercultural exchange. In R. O'Dowd & T. Lewis (Eds.), *Online intercultural exchange: Policy, pedagogy, practice* (pp. 150–172). New York, NY: Routledge.

Johnson, W. (2016). *On being a mentor: A guide for higher education faculty* (2nd ed.). New York, NY: Routledge.

Kolb, D. (2015). *Experiential learning: Experience as the source of learning and development* (2nd ed.). Upper Saddle River, NJ: Pearson.

Kuh, G. (2008). *High-impact educational practices: What they are, who has access to them, and why they matter.* Washington, DC: AAC&U.

Landorf, H., & Doscher, S. (2015). Defining global learning at Florida International University. *Diversity & Democracy, 18*(3), 24–25.

Leask, B. (2015). *Internationalizing the curriculum.* New York, NY: Routledge.

Merriam, S., Cafarella, R., & Baumgartner, L. (2007). *Learning in adulthood: A comprehensive guide* (3rd ed.). San Francisco, CA: Jossey-Bass.

Lewin, R. (Ed.). (2009). *The handbook of practice and research in study abroad: Higher education and the quest for global citizenship.* New York, NY: Routledge.

Lewis, T., & O'Dowd, R. (2016). Introduction to online intercultural exchange and this volume. In R. O'Dowd & T. Lewis (Eds.), *Online intercultural exchange: Policy, pedagogy, practice* (pp. 3–20). New York, NY: Routledge.

Müller-Hartmann, A., & Kurek, M. (2016). Virtual group formation and the process of task design in online intercultural exchanges. In R. O'Dowd & T. Lewis (Eds.), *Online intercultural exchange: Policy, pedagogy, practice* (pp. 131–149). New York, NY: Routledge.

Musil, C. (2006). *Assessing global learning: Matching good intentions with practice.* Association of American Colleges & Universities. Available at: archive.aacu.org/SharedFutures/documents/Global_Learning.pdf

Nair, I., & Henning, M. (2017). *Models of global learning.* Association of American Colleges and Universities. Available at: www.aacu.org/sites/default/files/files/publications/ModelsGlobalLearning.pdf

O'Grady, C. (2000). *Integrating service learning and multicultural education in colleges and universities.* Mahwah, NJ: Erlbaum.

Pless, N., Maak, T., & Stahl, G. (2011). Developing responsible global leaders through international service-learning programs: The Ulysses experience. *Academy of Management Learning & Education, 10*(2), 237–260.

Reimers, F. (2014). Bringing global education to the core of the undergraduate curriculum. *Diversity and Democracy, 17*(2). Available at: www.aacu.org/diversitydemocracy/2014/spring/reimers

Rubin, J. (2016). The collaborative online international learning network: Online intercultural exchange in the State University of New York Network of Universities. In R. O'Dowd & T. Lewis (Eds.), *Online intercultural exchange: Policy, pedagogy, practice* (pp. 263–270). New York, NY: Routledge.

State University of New York's Collaborative Online International Learning Network, or COIL (http://coil.suny.edu/). Example projects, a free guide for collaborative online projects (including assessment), and faculty training options.

Tarrant, M., Rubin, D., & Stoner, L. (2014). The added value of study abroad: Fostering a global citizenry. *Journal of Studies in International Education, 18*(2) 141–161.

Turner, Y., & Robson, S. (2008). *Internationalizing the university*. New York, NY: Continuum.

Wächter, B. (2003). An introduction: Internationalisation at home in context. *Journal of Studies in International Education, 7*(1) 5–11.

Whitehead, D. (2017). Foreword (pp. v–vi). In I. Nair & M. Henning (Eds.), *Models of global learning*. Association of American Colleges and Universities. Available at: www.aacu.org/sites/default/files/files/publications/ModelsGlobalLearning.pdf

Chapter 3

Communicating Within and Across Cultural Boundaries

 INTRODUCTION

In this chapter, we explore communication in educational experiences among diverse groups. Often referred to as intercultural communication, communicating with people who hold different perspectives or even have different appearances can affect our identities and appeal to our emotions, potentially making us feel interested and/or excited, but also potentially provoke anxiety, anger, fear, or self-doubt. When students are exposed to a new group (i.e., cultural or regional, gender, worldview), they can respond in a variety of ways: they can reject that new way of thinking, reject their own background and ways of thinking, go between the two, or synthesize the different perspectives into a new mindset. While accepting differences occurs at a cognitive level, it is often our emotions that help individuals become more interested in and curious about others. Becoming interculturally competent is, after all, "a process of changing one's mindset" and of "continuous transformation" (Guilherme, Glaser, & Méndez-García, 2010, pp. 243–244). Thus, the environment and rapport of a course and/or campus play a crucial role. This chapter provides strategies that faculty can use to help students develop their skills in communicating with people who are different from themselves.

By the end of this chapter, you should be able to:

- provide a broad definition of intercultural communication;
- explain what intercultural competence is and behaviors associated with it;
- discuss challenges and opportunities that come with communication among groups in an educational environment;
- be aware of potential differences in communication patterns that might affect our teaching and classrooms; and
- employ strategies to build students' intercultural communication skills in your context.

CLASSROOM AND SELF-ASSESSMENT

Before reading about intercultural communication and competence in depth, please reflect on your own teaching context and rate your students' abilities to engage in effective communication with people different from themselves. See the Preface for tips on assessing students' knowledge and values.

 ## ASSESSING HOW YOUR STUDENTS ARE DEVELOPING AS STRONG INTERCULTURAL COMMUNICATORS

Recognizing that some courses lend themselves more to helping students develop their intercultural communication skills than others, what opportunities does your course include for students to develop their communication skills with people different from themselves? Are there opportunities you might be missing?

By the time students leave my class/department, they:

0	actively avoid interacting with individuals from different backgrounds, groups, worldviews, or (sub-)cultures; engage in dialogue and actions that further stereotypes and misunderstandings; seek out like-minded individuals who hold similar damaging stereotypes.
★	neither avoid nor seek interaction with individuals from different backgrounds, groups, worldviews, or (sub-)cultures; may not hold strong damaging perceptions about other groups but do not challenge others to reconsider their stereotypes.
★★	are willing to interact with individuals from different backgrounds, groups, worldviews, or (sub-)cultures on a more superficial level (e.g., about foods, holidays, sports); have limited strategies to repair miscommunication or diffuse tensions related to misunderstandings in group situations.
★★★	actively seek out opportunities to interact with individuals from different backgrounds, groups, worldviews, or (sub-)cultures; can employ strategies to repair miscommunications or diffuse tensions related to misunderstandings, particularly in group situations; behave and communicate effectively and appropriately for the situation and to achieve their goals.

Example of a student at the two-star level: A student unintentionally offends a classmate of color during a small-group discussion. The student realizes their communication misstep, but is unaware of how to indicate that they meant no harm and that they value their classmate's perspective.

Example of a student at the three-star level: A student enters class the first day and chooses to sit near a group of classmates who appear to have different backgrounds. The student initiates conversations with them and also seeks to work with them during group work.

ASSESSING YOUR READINESS TO HELP STUDENTS DEVELOP INTERCULTURAL COMMUNICATION SKILLS

Faculty who have stronger intercultural communication skills are more able to assist students in this area. Not only do faculty members need to feel confident as intercultural communicators in these circumstances, but they also need to be willing and able to share their expertise with their students. While in some classrooms, topics more readily lend themselves to development in these areas, in other classrooms it is not the content that drives the opportunities for skill building, but rather the classroom atmosphere faculty create that embodies these values. Are there opportunities for you to expand your skills to help students demonstrate these ideals? The role or responsibility that departments perceive they play in assisting students in their development of intercultural communication skills affects individual faculty behaviors as well. This self-assessment can be answered from a personal or departmental perspective.

In my own teaching, I:

★	do not feel it is my responsibility to help students seek interaction with individuals from different backgrounds, groups, or (sub-)cultures. While I value this skill, it is outside the scope of our class to work on this in any way.
★ ★	can tell when students are not communicating across groups, but I am unsure of how to help them. I myself am not sure how to communicate across groups, particularly in educational contexts.
★ ★ ★	believe it is my responsibility to help students interact with others from different backgrounds. I feel comfortable with my level of intercultural communication and I have the skills to teach this to students by example, experience, and instruction.

Example of a faculty member at the three-star level: A faculty member in the natural sciences shares her class communication plan with her lab students. She explicitly states that students are expected to build not only their science content skills but also their communication skills. She trains students to communicate with diverse people and monitors student behavior, helping students work through potential miscommunication as needed.

The remaining sections in this chapter provide background information on intercultural communication, including areas of potential miscommunication. The chapter also provides strategies to help faculty a) raise student awareness about the importance of intercultural communication and intercultural competence, b) encourage students to develop their own intercultural competence, and c) support students in their development.

 ## KEY CONCEPTS

Our communication style and expectations are influenced by many factors: our backgrounds, culture, gender, age, ethnicity, member groups, languages, identities, and personality type. How we communicate is also influenced by power structures that exist between communicators and the groups they represent or find themselves in. These are some of the realities that make communication between groups fascinating learning opportunities on the one hand, yet on the other challenging, hard work. Developing intercultural communication skills takes practice, and at times it will be best to treat situations on a case-by-case basis. This section introduces key concepts, moving from intercultural communication in general to putting intercultural competence into action, with the understanding that communication skills require practice and are crucial not only in academia, but in the workplace as well (Guilherme, 2010).

Intercultural Communication

Intercultural communication can be described in many ways and is discussed in many fields (e.g., anthropology, communications, linguistics, psychology), but a simple and comprehensive definition is "communication between members of different groups" (Gudykunst, 2003, p. 163). This communication can occur face to face or via technology, in spoken or written form, and between people who differ not only across countries of origin or languages but also across gender or generational cultures, affinity groups, or identities (Scollon, Scollon, & Jones, 2012). Intercultural communication that tackles substantive issues can lead to deeper learning and even relationships built on mutual respect and an appreciation for diversity. More than a subject of academic study, intercultural communication is best experienced as a lived reality.

Very often, developing intercultural communication skills goes hand in hand with developing an identity. Going through intercultural experiences puts people in a vulnerable position and is often accompanied by the reconstruction of their worldviews, moving from an ethnocentric to geocentric awareness (Gerzon, 2010). Individuals who are more secure in their own identities are often more willing to experience this and communicate with diverse others (Ting-Toomey, 1993). The extent to which individuals are willing to work on their identities and yield to the transformative forces of intercultural experiences define the extent of the intercultural competence they may achieve.

Intercultural Competence

Increased intercultural competence is often cited as a result of university internationalization efforts. While institutions and scholars may utilize slightly different definitions of this term, one that is most widely agreed upon by scholars and administrators is "the ability to communicate effectively and appropriately in intercultural situations based on one's intercultural knowledge, skills, and attitudes" (Deardorff, 2006, p. 194). This definition includes outcomes that are both external (behavior-based) and internal (mindsets, attitudes). For many educators, intercultural competence is deemed crucial for an educated individual and an educated populace; many students, however, have not had the time or experiences to realize and value all that can be gained from communicating with people from different backgrounds. Students thus need time and opportunities to build awareness and skill in courses ranging from the humanities to the social sciences to science and technology. How each discipline contributes, in large or small ways, to a student's intercultural competence can be discussed at an institutional level to ensure that students are given the opportunities they need.

Characteristics of Intercultural Competence

Individuals with strong intercultural competence are more likely to be sensitive to cultural factors or differences and how those differences may affect communication and interpretations of meaning. A number of models from various fields related to intercultural communication and competence exist (e.g., Bennett & Bennett, 2004; Byram, 1997; Chen & Starosta, 2008; Deardorff, 2006; Guilherme et al., 2010). Practically speaking, individuals with strong intercultural communication skills:

- recognize that many concepts we take for granted are culturally based (e.g., politeness, logic, sense of time), leading to expectations and restraints;
- recognize that many actions or language acts are culturally based (e.g., greetings, requests, refusals, jokes);
- question their own responses before jumping to conclusions about the other person's intentions or the meaning of an action (e.g., reflecting instead of immediately taking offense at a very direct comment);

55

- have developed a set of skills and strategies to manage emotions that may arise from difference or ambiguity (Guilherme, 2010), thereby decreasing anxiety and focusing on meaning and humanity in communication; and
- can engage in intercultural dialogue (Anderson, 2010, in Killick, 2015) by demonstrating competence in listening and being willing to hear other perspectives; non-defensively appreciating others' accomplishments; disagreeing appropriately; and resolving conflicts.

Strong intercultural communicators are more likely to sit with individuals from different groups or volunteer to work with them in groups, or seek communication with instructors from different backgrounds. They seek and provide verbal and nonverbal feedback to ensure that messages were received as intended. When faced with potential communication breakdowns or disagreements, they focus on the other perspective and elicit stories or information that work toward understanding, a practice referred to as "silent yielding" by Jungkunz (2013).

The following *Student Voice* illustrates the complexity of developing intercultural competence and emphasizes the time and intentionality required for cultivating this mindset.

STUDENT VOICE: GAINING INTERCULTURAL COMPETENCE

Reflecting on my own intercultural experiences, I cannot stop thinking of the metaphor that gaining intercultural competence is like learning to walk. My intercultural journey started 13 years ago and is still in a full swing. I was a junior in my Ukrainian university when I left to the US for a one-year academic exchange. Crossing an ocean inevitably implied crossing a lot of other boundaries, as well as pushing my comfort zone. Despite a thorough preparation at the pre-departure and post-arrival orientations, my first year in the US in general, and studying at an American institution in particular, felt like learning to walk again.

It was a year full of excitement, eye-opening discoveries, new friendships, and life-changing transformations. However, it was also a year of frustration, tears, extreme homesickness (there was no Skype at that time, and international phone calls were expensive), academic challenges throughout the year (I got my first 'F' in life! after being a straight A student at home), and an overall emotionally taxing experience. I would never have traded it for anything else, but I can honestly admit that intercultural competence *in action* in the eyes of a 20-year-old was challenging. I still remember the thrill of excitement about going so far and doing something new. But I also remember the fear and uncertainty glaring at me as I was leaving my whole familiar life and world behind, going into a new culture.

After graduation from my Ukrainian alma mater, I gained more intercultural experience through travel and further developed the competence working in international organizations. I came back to the US to pursue my Master's degree eight years after my first visit. Interestingly, I thought I was ready by then, and that everything would go smoother the second time. Alas, no! It was, no doubt, easier; yet, the process was not easy. I had to meet new academic expectations, face the challenge of thinking/writing in a second (or third) language, and adjust to different communication patterns (small talk, for example, still challenges me conceptually and in practice).

For the third time in my life, I felt like I was learning to walk. This time, being able to walk was a more high-stakes endeavor since it wasn't an exchange year any more. Did I avoid falling this third time? Of course not. Did I still wonder at many things done in American class and outside of it? Quite often! Although Skype had become a part of life by then, was there a homesickness component present? Inevitably! And all these are very common challenges that international students may face.

My current "visit" to the US has proved to be the longest so far, approaching its fifth anniversary. I have learned some theory behind intercultural competence, attended various related workshops and conferences, and read the research about it. Yet, I am still "learning to walk" in a foreign culture. Intercultural competence can be developed and learned over time, but let us not underestimate the *time* needed for its cultivation, as well as the need for an *open mind*, and *intention to learn*. It is not an easy concept to grasp, even harder to internalize, and most difficult to externalize. This is why, every time I work with international students in the capacity of an academic advisor now, I pause, look back, and remember myself trying to learn to walk again.

Tetyana Dovbnya
Former international student and International
Academic Advisor for the College of Arts
and Sciences Ohio University

Tetyana Dovbnya's description of developing intercultural competence is moving, showing the emotional complexities of a journey that can feel isolating and almost insurmountable. Students having the opportunity to share their stories allows them to build their confidence and connect with others. Also, hearing personal stories allows faculty to develop a more comprehensive understanding of the types of support that diverse students may need. Connecting with students is one strategy that faculty can use to develop their own confidence and understanding with intercultural competence.

Supporting Intercultural Competence

Faculty who are comfortable with their own intercultural communication skills will be most prepared to support students in these areas. Qualities of strong intercultural communicators overlap with those of a global citizen in the areas of knowledge, skills, and attitudes. Faculty and staff wanting to develop in these areas are encouraged to consider the following:

- *Knowledge*: Are you able to explain how your field operates on a global level (e.g., with global examples, case studies, relevance) and the knowledge that intercultural communicators need in order to engage in appropriate and substantive communication? Are you aware of resources to support students as they seek to develop their intercultural communication skills? Are you comfortable pronouncing names of students from different countries? While practicing, try: "Let me try to get your name right" or "Please correct me while I try to learn that pronunciation."
- *Skills*: Can you provide examples that help students make connections between their own learning and how their actions can have global implications? Are you able to help students reflect on their own learning and communication through examples that feature diversity or various worldviews? Do you have strategies for helping less vocal students share their ideas or participate in class (e.g., through media such as discussion boards, blogs, videos, a teacher-only discussion area)?
- *Attitudes*: Are you aware of the role that cultural assumptions play in identity and communication and are you willing to question those assumptions? Are you comfortable with difference in the classroom? Do you work to identify your biases and keep them in check? Can you articulate benefits related to intercultural communication?

The following *Case Study* suggests possible reasons students choose not to share openly in class, and explores options that faculty have in respecting their privacy while also upholding expectations of participation and engagement.

CASE STUDY: BRINGING OUR CULTURES TO CLASS

One of my recent students was a Chinese woman who never spoke in class at all. She completed her work and was quite proficient, but she never volunteered information in class. Since I wasn't sure of her speaking proficiency and comfort, I didn't call on her.

Then she came to my office for one of the mandatory conferences I have for each paper. It turned out that she was very articulate and highly engaged with the class material; however, she was also Communist and this had generated conflict with her peers when she had participated in other classes. She was adamant that she would not speak in class. In this particular case, I chose not to push her and let her demonstrate her engagement through blog postings and conferences, even though that meant the rest of the class didn't get to hear her perspective. I never would have known she was so engaged without those mandatory conferences though.

Dr. Talinn Phillips
Associate Professor of English
Ohio University

Both the *Student Voice* and *Case Study* showcase the complexities and internal component of intercultural communication. They also showcase the role of language as a powerful force in our communication, demonstrating the need for students to be able to choose wording that facilitates understanding and opens the door for mutual respect and dialogue.

Intercultural Competence and Language

Be prepared for students to make intentionally or unintentionally disrespectful or offensive comments in class. It is usually best to not ignore the comment or the reality that some students may be offended. Instead of labeling the student or making light humor in the situation, faculty can: redirect the discussion to a less heated topic; encourage students to question any assumptions they have that led to the comment; encourage everyone to write, instead of verbally share, their feelings; or, if necessary, work with students outside of class. Gauging student interest in pursuing the discussion at that time or in the future is key as well.

Helping students build their intercultural communication skills often involves supplying them with the words and ideas they need to discuss these complicated issues. Language that can be useful to incorporate into materials, discussions, and group projects can be broken into three broad categories: language to use, language to avoid, and language to consider.

Language to Use

- *Language of inclusivity:* Model language that indicates inclusivity, respect, and appreciation of other perspectives. Examples include: "That's interesting, I never thought of it that way" or "Thanks for that perspective; it really makes me think." Rephrasing a student comment into more inclusive wording establishes expectations without unnecessary confrontation.

- *Language of respectful disagreement:* Model language on how to respectfully disagree. Examples include: "While I see your point, I would also like to point out that…" or "That's an interesting perspective, but in fact it's very different from what I've experienced. In my case…" In this way, students can gain confidence in expressing their opinions while also minimizing concerns about conflict in communication.

- *Language against stereotypes and discrimination:* Language that takes a respectful stand against stereotypes and discrimination is crucial. For example: "There are other ways to think about that point, such as…" Unfortunately, language that calls out problematic behavior or statements is occasionally necessary as well. Examples include using "I" statements to express how racist remarks affect one's feelings, or asking the individual to consider the situation from another point of view (e.g., "If this happened to you, what would you do or how would you feel?"). If necessary, students can be told that racist or discriminatory remarks are unacceptable in the classroom; whenever possible, it is best to lead them to understand how their remarks affect others.

Language to Avoid

- *Culturally loaded or offensive language:* Many words should be avoided because they may offend others or give the wrong impression. Besides obviously inappropriate slurs, unintentional examples include terms such as "poor people" or using race- or ethnic-based descriptions (e.g., "Asian" instead of the more specific "someone from Japan" or "Japanese individual").

- *Overly general and potentially insulting language or questions:* Statements that overly generalize a group of people and appear to discount individuality should be avoided (e.g., "You people" or "Those people"). It's also important to avoid statements that assume that all members of a community eat certain foods, wear certain clothing, or practice certain behaviors or beliefs. These microaggressions (i.e., seemingly minor comments that express often unconscious prejudices and whose impact compounds over time for diverse people) can occur quickly and often unintentionally, for example through questions such as "Where are you *really* from?" or comments suggesting that an individual doesn't behave in a stereotypical manner.

Language to Consider

- *Potentially loaded language:* Being aware of terms or phrases that represent hot-button issues allows educators to choose their words carefully and with an awareness of audience. While to some, "diversity" represents an unmistakably positive value, to others this term represents a type of reverse discrimination; diversity initiatives have resulted in some people feeling left behind. The term "white privilege" to many indicates an awareness of how race allows some groups to reap almost invisible benefits based on skin color alone, while others resent the term and interpret is as referring to economic privileges which they feel they don't enjoy.

Assessing Intercultural Competence

Faculty and administrators can assess students' intercultural competence through both quantitative and qualitative means, such as student interviews, papers, presentations, portfolios, or self-reports; observations of student behavior; professor evaluation; or pre-test/post-test instruments (Deardorff, 2006). Commercial and free scales to measure intercultural competence are available as well (see this chapter's bibliography). Many models to assess intercultural competence can be accessed by faculty or administrators for courses or curricula, such as Byram's (1997) *Savoirs*, the Intercultural Assessment Project (see Lund & O'Regan, 2010), and the Association of American Colleges and Universities' Intercultural Knowledge and Competence VALUE Rubric (www. aacu.org/value-rubrics). Contemporary assessment of intercultural competence focuses more on competences and multiple identities found within local groups than on differences between national cultures (Lund & O'Regan, 2010). These assessments can be used to guide goal setting for course development and for in-class communication.

For faculty interested in leading self-assessment or reflective activities with their students, the following *Case Study* describes one option. This professor encourages her students to reflect on their own identities and build an understanding of how others perceive them in order to further develop their intercultural competence.

CASE STUDY: ANALYZING OUR OWN IDENTITY

I have an exercise I like to use to help students assess the multidimensionality of their identities and the dialectics between self and other. This assignment has three parts: a) the students answer a few questions about themselves to understand their own selves; b) then they ask the same questions to two people who are close to them to find what they think about them; and c) they write a short essay combining the two sets of responses to illustrate the multidimensionality of one's identity, the dialectics between their self-concept, and how others view them.

I. Analyzing Self

Objective: Describing self. How do we view ourselves?
1. List ten words that describe you.
2. Describe in your own words your physical appearance.
3. When you think of yourself, do you think that you belong to a certain race, ethnicity, or religious group?
4. What skills do you possess? In other words, what skills come naturally to you?
5. Explain your communication patterns in your interactions with others.
6. What work ethics/characteristics do you possess?

II. How Others View Us

Objective: Evaluate how others view you.
   Directions: Talk to two people who know you well and ask them these questions. Jot down the answers.
1. List ten words to describe you.
2. Describe your physical appearance.
3. When they think of you, do they think that you belong to a certain race, ethnicity, or religious group?
4. What skills do they think you possess? In other words, what skills come naturally to you?
5. Explain how they view your communication patterns when you interact with others.
6. What work ethics/characteristics do they think you possess?

III. How Perceptions of Identities Compare

After students gather information on their own identity and how others view them, they write a short essay combining the information they gather. I ask them to consider and give examples of the multidimensionality of their identity, including the similarities or differences between their self-concept and how others view them.

> When students participate in this activity, they often realize so many things about themselves that they had previously never noticed. And they realize that how they view others is just a fraction of that person's identity as well.
>
> Dr. Purba Das
> *Associate Professor of Communication Studies*
> *Ohio University-Southern*

Purba Das's activity highlights the tension that can occur between how we perceive ourselves vs. how we are perceived by others. Another way to have students visualize often invisible components of who we are is to have them create and reflect on *identity pyramids* (moving from least- to most-salient identity components) or *identity pies* with pieces representing who they are (race or ethnicity, gender, socioeconomic class, religion, values, hobbies). Using the information they gain from understanding their own identities, students can be encouraged to increase their empathy for others in addition to experiment with different communication styles that may more closely align with their intentions. The following strategies continue to explore ways to help students engage with and learn from people different from themselves.

 ## CLASSROOM STRATEGIES

Three questions on how to support intercultural communication follow, ranging from raising student awareness, to variations in communication styles, to leading students through miscommunication.

"How can I guide students to notice how their communication is influenced by their culture and background?"

- During discussions, ask students to reflect on why they hold a particular perspective. Guide them into questioning their own biases and notice how the language they use and their communication patterns reveal those ideas.
- Arrange course activities that require collaboration or communication between diverse groups of students. Push them to notice how others' communication is affected by their culture and, ultimately, how their own is as well.
- Case studies or film segments provide a way for students to discuss influences on their communication in an atmosphere that is less threatening

yet retains a realistic perspective. Students can choose to discuss personal experiences within the framework of the case.

- Students from some groups may benefit from being reminded that they may want to establish credibility at the beginning of interactions, for example by sharing their expertise, in order to facilitate smoother communication.

"How might students from different backgrounds communicate differently, both verbally and nonverbally?"

Students who come from different backgrounds may have different communication styles. This can include those from different countries or even regions within the same country, from various ethnic backgrounds, from different age groups or genders, or with differing worldviews. Being aware of possible differences allows faculty to monitor classroom dynamics and make informed choices when structuring learning.

1. Eye Contact and Proximity

For some, it is rude to look a teacher in the eye; if a student looks at the floor or away they may be showing respect or just may not be comfortable with eye contact. Looking away does not necessarily signify rudeness or disinterest. Similarly, expectations regarding physical proximity during communication can vary between groups.

2. Facial Expressions

In some cultures, listeners put on a less expressive facial expression. This does not necessarily mean the person is not listening or is bored. This nonverbal behavior difference can be difficult for educators as well as domestic students. Even when or why individuals smile is often influenced by culture.

3. Directness and/or Formality of Communication

Directness and formality can vary greatly between groups and also provide the potential for considerable miscommunication, tension, or conflict. While some individuals may ask questions directly, for example, others may state a fact and assume the listener will understand the implicit question. In some cultures, stating a preference is less accepted, with individuals using "maybe" when they really mean "no," whereas in other groups few softening comments are ever used. Directness of communication can be affected by other factors, such as gender, as well. Similarly, some groups expect more formal communication and can become confused or even offended if informal language is directed at them. Communicators can thus be perceived as intentionally rude or vague even if this was not their intent.

4. Displays of Outward Confidence or Openness to Communication

While some students feel more comfortable displaying confidence in sharing their opinions, to others this behavior can seem pushy or unfamiliar. These differences can be based on personality, background, age, or gender. Students from some countries in the Middle East, for example, may not be used to interacting with members of the opposite gender and may need support in their class participation. Or, males from any culture may dominate class discussions, leaving little room for female students to voice their comments. Some groups are more comfortable with silence and use it as part of their communication.

5. Apparent Motivation

While most classes have at least a few seemingly unmotivated students, it can be challenging to determine their actual interest level. Collecting evidence of student work in various formats can be helpful. For example, call on them to determine if they are paying attention, talk to them before/after class, or pair them up with animated students and monitor their response. For groups of seemingly unmotivated students who are negatively affecting class dynamics, try talking to them as a group and eliciting their feedback as well as providing clear guidelines and expectations of class behavior.

"What are some strategies to try if miscommunication occurs?"

It's helpful to first consider circumstances or values that seem to trigger miscommunication. For example, miscommunication can occur when two communicators have different perceptions about what is a polite or impolite topic of conversation or statements that are overly direct or too indirect. Nonverbal communication such as eye contact can trigger misunderstandings as well. Once students realize what may have triggered the miscommunication, they can problem-solve with repair strategies.

1. Language and communication repair strategies can include:
- repeating information;
- restating information in a different way; and

- using nonverbal communication, such as demonstrating patience through body language.

2. Cultural repair strategies can include:
   - maintaining a positive attitude with minimal frustration;
   - actively listening and looking for meaning;
   - identifying the potential miscommunication trigger;
   - rethinking the situation from the other's perspective in order to reframe the conversation;
   - explaining any potential misunderstanding using "I-statements" and avoiding accusatory statements;
   - avoiding overly emotional or inflammatory messages; and
   - seeking assistance if necessary.

Students can be reminded of the importance of practice in their skill building by relating examples from non-communication tasks. Decorating a cake, for example, requires practice; students can be shown two cakes, one after practicing several times and the other a first-time attempt. As students realize that practice and increased exposure to diverse communication situations will help them build their strategies, they can gain the confidence they need to work through miscommunication challenges.

The following *Case Study* explores the complexity of intercultural communication not only between students, or between faculty and students, but in this case also between international teaching assistants (TAs) and their domestic undergraduate students, many of whom have limited intercultural experiences.

CASE STUDY: INTERNATIONAL STUDENTS AS TEACHERS AND LEARNERS

Years ago, I was an international student and also an international teaching assistant. While the American culture was not new to me, I had to adapt to the education system, which was quite different from the one I was used to. What I found so difficult was how public the struggles of international teaching assistants can be—we have to live our culture shock in the classrooms where we learn and also where we teach. How we were taught is often how we approach teaching, meaning that many of the international TAs struggle with designing classes that are student-focused and interactive. I have seen international TAs facing a variety of issues such as bringing culture into the classroom; social hierarchies; expectations for respect and formality; the place of religion in public spaces; and pacing, time management, and workload.

Now, as a TA supervisor, I can see that while students from some cultures might be more comfortable interacting with all kinds of people, students from other cultures seem to have a harder time adapting, resorting to interacting with people from their home country only. Some of these students experience loneliness and this gradually affects their performance. Our international teaching assistants don't know the types of things that may be taken for granted here in the US, such as how to keep track of the climate in our classes or how to provide support and individualized attention. We can offer a variety of types of support to them, including orientations that are longer and more involved, courses on teaching methods, weekly support meetings, student midterm evaluations, peer mentoring, and spaces (e.g., blogs) to share their experiences and what they've learned. Being an international student myself and now working in the university, I've learned about the struggles we can all have and that often are invisible. Increased dialog, listening, and understanding among all of us on campus is crucial.

Dr. Muriel Gallego
Associate Professor of Modern Languages,
Director of First Year Spanish, and TA Coordinator
Ohio University

Muriel Gallego's description showcases the needs of international TAs, which are often overlooked on campus. As they experience transformation and development in their intercultural competence, extra attention may be needed to help them identify and meet the requirements for their teaching as well.

 THE WORKSHOP

3.1 Assessing Students' Intercultural Competence

Students' levels of intercultural competence can be measured qualitatively or quantitatively. A useful first step for the classroom is to qualitatively measure their level at the beginning of a term and then later in the semester or year. Work from each student can be collected and assessed or, for larger classes, samples from a smaller number of students can be utilized.

Review the AAC&U's Intercultural Knowledge and Competence VALUE Rubric (available at: www.aacu.org/value-rubrics). Choose two or three areas to focus on out of the six available (cultural self-awareness, knowledge of cultural worldviews, empathy, verbal and nonverbal communication, curiosity, and openness). Identify and gather student work that can be evaluated using the rubric. Options include student interviews, papers, presentations, portfolios, or self-reports; observations of student behavior; or professor evaluation. Complete the table below for the beginning and ending of the time period you chose, gathering data throughout.

Areas of Intercultural Communication Focus	Student Work	Initial Level	End Level

Reflect on your students' progress and future opportunities, as well as strategies you may be able to include in the future to help students to develop further. This can be within one course or over several courses.

3.2 Intervening to Build Successful Intercultural Communication

Communication breakdowns can often be overwhelming in the moment. Practicing possible responses can help you feel better prepared if you need to respond "on your feet." Read through the three scenarios below in which you witness a communication breakdown among your students. For each situation, consider the following four main areas:

- **How to Respond**—How can you respond in a way that avoids embarrassing students but also minimizes the chances that such a problem occurs again? What needs to be communicated and to whom? What tone will be most constructive? What alternatives can you offer to future students? Do you need to make changes to your classroom activities or instructions to avoid this problem in the future?

- **When to Respond**—Is this situation best dealt with immediately during class, privately after class, or in a couple of days after everyone has had a chance to cool off or recover?
- **What Medium to Use to Respond**—Should you talk to someone face to face, make a phone call, or send an email? Is the situation serious enough that you need to involve some other office on campus such as Institutional Equity or campus police?
- **How Your Ideas Change Based on the Student Population**— Do you have different ideas (or can you draw on different experiences) depending on how you imagine the demographics of the students (e.g., a domestic student of color, a domestic white student, an international student, a student who is obviously poorer than most students in class)?

You might also examine how your response changes based on the demographics of the students involved. Try rolling a dice and assigning students some demographic characteristics based on the key below:

1 represents an international student from East Asia
2 represents a student with a disability
3 represents a domestic, white student
4 represents a student of color
5 represents a student who is obviously poorer than most students in the class
6 represents an international student from the Middle East.

Scenarios

1. *The Exclusive Group*

You've given your class a collaborative assignment and put them into groups. As you observe the working of the groups during class time, you notice that Student A is sitting on the edge of the group and that no one is talking to her or including her in the discussion of the group's plans. How would you help Student A be included?

Your response:

2. *The Racist Comment*

As you're about to finish class, Student A raises a hand and asks a question that has strong racist undertones. Many students in the room are visibly shocked. Student A seems to have asked the question innocently enough and doesn't seem to be aware that the question was offensive.

Your response:

3. *The Hostile Feedback*

Students have been put into pairs to give each other feedback on their projects. You overhear Student A giving feedback to Student B: "But why should I care about your project? I'm just saying, it's not interesting to me and I don't see what the point is." His tone strikes you as very dismissive and the student who was given the feedback looks angry.

Your response:

3.3 Observing Communication in the Classroom

Considering possible communication breakdown scenarios (Workshop 3.2) can inform classroom observations. Observe students communicating (in your class or a colleague's class) and consider how you may want to intervene to help them improve their intercultural communication or how you might structure activities to help students develop these skills. Try observing groups of students who are diverse in some way. Take note of their nonverbal behavior and body language, facial expressions, individual speaking time, eye contact, topic control, frustrations, or excitement.

Write observations you notice about students' intercultural communication skills. What strategies can you try in the moment or include in future classes or assignments to help them develop their skills? A sample comment is included below.

Observations on students' intercultural communication skills:	Ways to help students develop their intercultural communication skills and intercultural competence:
For more vocal students: • *Some students have strong communication skills but are hesitant to use them with people unlike themselves*	

Observations on students' intercultural communication skills:	Ways to help students develop their intercultural communication skills and intercultural competence:
For less vocal students: • •	
For students who may be frustrated: • •	
Other:	

 DISCUSSION AND REFLECTION

1. How would you describe yourself and your identity? Conversely, what are some descriptors of what you are not? How might your sense of self affect your teaching and communication with diverse groups in your classes?

2. In what areas might you want to better prepare yourself to be a more comfortable leader or facilitator for intercultural groups or discussions? This could be related to knowledge you would like to build, skills related to intercultural communication, or attitudes you would like to encourage in your students, etc.

3. What little things might you be able to do in your own educational context to make groups of students more comfortable interacting when it can be messy or frustrating?

4. In many cultures, indirect communication is valued over direct communication. Have you been in a situation where you needed to be more indirect when you are a more direct communicator? Discuss the challenges that communicating in this different manner presents. What unique challenges do indirect communicators encounter in our direct classrooms and how might we help facilitate this transition?

5. Are institutional resources sufficiently supporting goals of helping students increase their intercultural communication skills? Who is tasked with this in your context? If no one, are there pathways to raising this discussion topic in your institution?

6. Are there opportunities for collaboration between faculty and students to discuss student expectations, perspectives, and support needed as they build their intercultural competence? For example, could your institution host a forum series or global dialogue for students to share their thoughts?

 BIBLIOGRAPHY

Bennett, J., & Bennett, M. (2004). Developing intercultural sensitivity: An integrative approach to global and domestic diversity. In D. Landis, J. Bennett, & M. Bennett (Eds.), *Handbook of intercultural training* (3rd ed., pp. 145–167). Thousand Oaks, CA: Sage.

Byram, M. (1997). *Teaching and assessing intercultural communicative competence.* Clevedon, UK: Multilingual Matters.

Chen, G., & Starosta, W. (2008). *Foundations of intercultural communication.* Needham Height, MA: Allyn and Bacon.

Deardorff, D. (2006). Identification and assessment of intercultural competence as a student outcome of internationalization. *Journal of Studies in International Education, 10*(3), 241–266.

Gerzon, M. (2010). *Global citizens: How our vision of the world is outdated, and what we can do about it.* London, UK: Rider.

Gudykunst, W. (2003). Intercultural communication. In W. Gudykunst (Ed.), *Cross-cultural and intercultural communication* (pp. 163–166). Thousand Oaks, CA: Sage.

Guilherme, M. (2010). Introduction. In M. Guilherme, E. Glaser, & M. Méndez-García (Eds.), *The intercultural dynamics of multicultural working* (pp. 1–17). Bristol, UK: Multilingual Matters.

Guilherme, M., Glaser, E., & Méndez-García, M. (2010). Conclusion: Intercultural competence for professional mobility. In M. Guilherme, E. Glaser, & M. Méndez-García (Eds.), *The intercultural dynamics of multicultural working* (pp. 241–245). Bristol, UK: Multilingual Matters.

Intercultural Effectiveness Scale (www.kozaigroup.com/intercultural-effectiveness-scale-ies/). Evaluates how effectively someone can interact with people from different cultures or backgrounds.

Jungkunz, V. (2013). Deliberate silences. *Journal of Public Deliberation, 9*(1), Article 12. Available at: www.publicdeliberation.net/jpd/vol9/iss1/art12

Killick, D. (2015). *Developing the global student: Higher education in an era of globalization.* London, UK: Routledge.

Lund, A., & O'Regan, J. (2010). National occupational standards in intercultural working: Models of theory and assessment. In M. Guilherme, E. Glaser, & M. Méndez-García (Eds.), *The intercultural dynamics of multicultural working* (pp. 41–58). Bristol, UK: Multilingual Matters.

Scollon, R., Scollon, S., & Jones, R. (2012). *Intercultural communication: A discourse approach* (3rd ed.). Malden, MA: Wiley.

The Developmental Model of Intercultural Sensitivity (www.idrinstitute.org/page. asp?menu1=15). Framework intended to "explain how people experience and engage cultural difference."

The Intercultural Development Continuum (https://idiinventory.com/products/the-intercultural-development-continuum-idc/). Adapted from the Developmental Model of Intercultural Sensitivity and situates various knowledge areas, attitudes, and skills along a continuum.

Thiagarajan, S., & Thiagarajan, R. (2006). *Barnga: A simulation game on cultural clashes* (3rd ed.). Boston, MA: Intercultural Press. Simulation game that allows players to improve their intercultural communication skills.

Tiltfactor Games for Social Change (www.tiltfactor.org/). Games that seek to promote learning and change in attitudes and behaviors, such as reducing stereotypes and increasing global awareness.

Ting-Toomey, S. (1993). Communicative resourcefulness: An identity negotiation theory. In R. Wiseman & J. Koester (Eds.), *Intercultural communication competence* (pp. 72–111). Newbury Park, CA: Sage.

Part II

Curricula, Course, and Assignment Design

Chapter 4

Designing Curricula and Courses That Foster Global Citizens

 INTRODUCTION

Having laid out important concepts that underlie teaching with a global perspective, we now consider the details of how to plan learning experiences that will both challenge and support all students as they develop global perspectives. We begin broadly in this chapter, exploring how faculty can design courses that not only maximize the potential for students to develop a global perspective, but that also allow students from a variety of backgrounds to feel included and engaged in course content. First, we surface the many different ways that "curriculum" manifests on our campus. Faculty most readily think of curriculum of their individual classes, but we need to look beyond our own classes, analyzing the messages that our programmatic, co-curricular, and extracurricular activities convey to our students.

We address several fundamental principles and concepts underlying effective course design such as alignment, the use of learning outcomes, and Universal Design for Learning. We also highlight some particularly effective pedagogies such as active learning and learner-centered activities. Though there is much more that could be said on all of these topics, our aim in this chapter is to introduce these important ideas to those who may not have encountered them before and to highlight how these particular classroom choices foster a global perspective.

By the end of this chapter, you should be able to:

- identify learner-centered, active approaches to learning and how to incorporate more of them into your own teaching;
- identify and discuss ways to develop or revise curricula to foster a global perspective;
- identify examples of formal, informal, and hidden curricula and how they influence students;
- craft meaningful global learning outcomes; and
- identify and discuss characteristics of assignments that encourage students to develop a global perspective and feelings of inclusivity.

CLASSROOM AND SELF-ASSESSMENT

Before reading the *Key Concepts*, begin by reflecting on course design and how it can affect students' degree of inclusion and the development of a global perspective. For ideas on how to assess students' knowledge and values, see the Preface.

 ## ASSESSING HOW YOUR COURSE DESIGN HELPS STUDENTS BECOME GLOBAL CITIZENS

When all students feel they can call on their own backgrounds and experiences to succeed in the course, they are in a more open position to develop a global perspective. Do your students feel that their perspectives and experiences are welcome in the class and benefit the class as a whole? Are there opportunities to increase feelings of inclusion that you might be missing?

In my courses:

★	Students have few opportunities to utilize their own backgrounds or experiences for class assignments or assessments; they are not explicitly asked to demonstrate knowledge or communication skills that would indicate a global perspective.
★★	Students have opportunities to utilize their own backgrounds or experiences for class assignments or assessments, but the opportunities tend to prioritize one group or culture over others, meaning that some students may feel excluded; they are explicitly asked to demonstrate knowledge or communication skills that would indicate a global perspective, but these skills are not assessed.
★★★	Students from diverse backgrounds have opportunities to utilize their own backgrounds or experiences for class assignments or assessments and are encouraged to do so; students are explicitly asked to demonstrate knowledge or communication skills that would indicate a global perspective, and these skills are assessed.

Example of a course at the three-star level: A Muslim, Indonesian student in a Women's and Gender Studies course chooses to examine the role of women as armed combatants in her home province, a role that her classmates and teacher hadn't known exists. She thinks her classmates would enjoy one of the readings she's found on the topic and suggests it to the teacher, who asks the class to read and discuss it. On the midterm, students are asked to respond to "What is a feminist?" from a variety of racial, national, and/or ethnic perspectives (e.g., Gloria Steinem, Julia Kristeva, Chimamanda Ngozi Adichie, Audre Lorde).

KEY CONCEPTS

The literature of pedagogy and course design is extensive; thus, our focus in these *Key Concepts* is introducing a handful of fundamental concepts that are particularly useful for fostering a global perspective.

Curricula and the Student Experience

In examining curricula, it's first important to recognize that there are always multiple levels of curriculum in operation and that an individual faculty member typically won't have control over every level. When institutions use the word "curriculum," they typically refer to the *formal curriculum*, or the official teaching and learning activities of a course—the syllabus, learning objectives, textbooks, assessments—and then how each of those elements play out within a particular course. They're also referring to how different courses work together to achieve learning outcomes for a major, certificate, etc. The formal curriculum is communicated to students explicitly and typically in ways that are highly formalized themselves. For example, the syllabus becomes an official contract between the instructor and the class and typically must be kept on file.

In addition to the formal curriculum, each institution also has an *informal curriculum*, which includes (frequently optional) experiences like conferences, lectures, films, etc. These opportunities influence the campus climate, but they are likely planned/sponsored by many different groups to support many different goals and thus lack any significant coherency. The informal curriculum also may not be assessed in any way. While some students may participate in many activities in the informal curriculum, job and family commitments may mean that others never do. An individual faculty member may have minimal influence over an institution's informal curriculum.

Finally, each institution, program, and teacher also has a *hidden curriculum*, or an organization's culture and the accompanying, often unspoken messages about values, preferred behaviors, and characteristics. Sambell and McDowell (1998) describe it as "the shadowy, ill-defined, and amorphous nature [...] which is implicit and embedded in educational experiences" (pp. 391–392). One facet of the hidden curriculum is norms, which are frequently white, hetero, and middle class. Faculty are implicitly recognizing the hidden curriculum when a student transgresses a norm in some way, for example by using texting abbreviations in formal academic writing, coming into class very late without offering an apology or explanation, addressing professors by their first names (without an invitation), or giving professors extravagant or otherwise inappropriate gifts. These actions often leave us feeling hurt ("How could they have been so rude?"), frustrated ("Do I really have to explain that showing up

79

to class 30 minutes late is inappropriate?"), or trapped in an awkward situation. Moreover, the hidden curriculum cuts across contexts and student populations. Acker (2001) painfully describes the disconnects between graduate students looking for dissertation directors and the faculty they (inappropriately and thus unsuccessfully) approach because no one has articulated the norms to them.

Yet what these situations really reveal is who is an academic "insider" and who is an "outsider." While faculty often experience the hidden curriculum as basic politeness, those politeness norms are culturally driven. Students from other cultures don't always share the norms that dominate many US institutions. For example, cultural notions of time vary widely; a student who came to class 30 minutes late may have felt that this was a sign of respect compared with the disrespect of not coming to class at all. Gift-giving norms vary as well. One of our faculty learning community participants described receiving a gift from a student. The student was female, the gift was a heart-shaped box of chocolates, and she gave the gift on Valentine's Day. As a recently arrived African immigrant, she was most likely unaware of and did not intend the many awkward, unspoken messages that accompanied her gift. Cultures also have different "rules of engagement" about discussion and expressing a point of view. The student who seems to be constantly arguing in class may belong to a culture where passionate engagement is a marker of a just cause. Or, the student may have a disability that makes it difficult to read other's nonverbal cues of discomfort.

Another tool for identifying hidden curriculum is to examine what receives time and attention. For instance, our formal curriculum might emphasize the development of higher-order thinking skills while the truth of the hidden curriculum is that every assessment is a fill-in-the-blank test. Or, compare the implicit messages of English Department A, which offers a single, elective course called "Diverse Authors" every other year to English Department B, which offers ten different courses on the literatures and rhetorics of minority cultural groups and requires at least four of these courses for the major. Department B has clearly committed much more time and resources to understanding and including minority cultures; they also communicate a clear value that these cultures are important by ensuring that students encounter multiple cultures in order to graduate. In contrast, Department A has lumped all other cultures around the globe into "Diverse Authors," sending strong messages of tokenism and that the "real work" of an English Department is Anglo culture.

Ultimately, the hidden curriculum tends to reinforce existing stereotypes, inequalities, and the status quo by indicating the knowledge and experiences that are most privileged. Thus, students from minority groups may experience hidden curriculum as marginalization and exclusion. What signals do we send to students if our websites, newsletters, textbooks, and public art only show people who are white, straight, and middle class? Or male? Or speaking English as a home language? Or are "Temporarily Able-Bodied"?

For global learning to occur, we need curricula that are "equitable, respectful and inclusive" (Killick, 2015, p. 2). This necessitates pulling back the curtain on the hidden curriculum. What coursework, concepts, or narratives are prioritized in terms of time or assessment? In what ways does your class work to de-center dominant and hegemonic perspectives? The more time a student experiences in an educational system that has a monocultural hidden curriculum, the more reinforced and damaging that point of view becomes.

The Workshop explores how we can recognize elements of the informal or hidden curriculum that might need changing. The following *Case Study* describes how one teacher's cross-cultural experience helped her to recognize an element of the hidden curriculum in both cultures.

CASE STUDY: TRAVEL AS A TEACHER OF TIME

I had the honor of representing my university during the graduation ceremony of a hybrid program offered by my institution to students at a Ghanaian university. During my weeklong stay, I followed the schedule prepared for me, designed so that I would meet various university officials and explore the possibility of future collaborations.

I quickly noticed that the real start time for most meetings was 20–90 minutes later than indicated on the schedule. Sometimes start times were delayed because the key person had not yet arrived, and other times the key person was already in the room with someone else or other people occupied the designated meeting room. In either case, those who were to attend the meeting would congregate—usually standing—in the hallway and enjoy relaxed conversation.

During meetings people would come and go. It was not uncommon for people to answer a cell phone call during the meeting and conduct part of a conversation before leaving the room. When a high ranking person would enter the room, people would momentarily stop the present conversation to greet the individual—in a group as large as 15 to 20 the high ranking person would go around the table giving hug, handshake, or pat on the shoulder to each attendee—and then the meeting would continue.

The penultimate example of the difference between how American and Ghanaian cultures treat time came on graduation day. The outdoor ceremony was scheduled for 10:00 a.m., so my American colleague and I showed up to campus at 9:30 a.m. with our regalia. As students and faculty gathered and 10:00 was nearing, we donned our caps and gowns—it was 80° Fahrenheit—and gathered near where the faculty procession would begin. Long story short: the processional began nearly 3 hours later. Students' families entered the commencement grounds over the 3-hour period, and the time of waiting seemed entirely natural with no one looking at watches or asking what the hold-up was. We all stood for that time—with few shade trees and no benches or chairs available—and engaged in friendly conversation. Once all the guests were seated, the Vice Chancellor led in the procession of faculty and graduating students, and the remainder of the ceremony turned out to be quite formal, much like I'd experienced in the US.

Dr. Linda J. Rice
Professor of English
Ohio University

Linda Rice's experience of Ghana could have been one of frustration because "nothing ever started on time." Instead, she recognized that there were different cultural norms operating and that her Ghanaian hosts placed less value on "starting on time" than is typical in the United States. She was able to identify this value in the hidden curriculum and adapt to it instead of becoming frustrated and possibly offending her hosts.

Learner-centered and Active Teaching

In exploring course and assignment design, our primary emphasis is approaches to learning that are *learner*-centered, or educational practices that shift the focus and power in the classroom from the teacher to students, and practices that are *active*, requiring students "to do meaningful learning activities and think about what they are doing" (Prince, 2004, p. 223). We emphasize these approaches, which often overlap, in contrast to traditional, lecture-based instruction. This is not because lecturing is never appropriate or has no value, but because it is, in general, less effective than learner-centered and active approaches (Prince, 2004; Weimer, 2013). Additionally, learner-centered and active learning pedagogies are more adept at de-centering a monocultural perspective, encouraging diverse students to contribute to the class, and facilitating intercultural communication. This is not to say that learner-centered or active learning is a magic wand, but it does offer more possibilities for facilitating a global perspective than a lecture-based course with multiple-choice assessments.

Active learning is a broad term that, as Prince (2004) points out, encompasses a wide range of pedagogical activities and thus gets defined quite broadly. Prince's (2004) meta-analysis of active learning research revealed that having students do essentially anything other than sit and listen to a lecture produced better results. Active learning includes pair work, group work, problem-solving, researching, debating, writing, presenting, and more.

Learner-centered classrooms also encompass a wide variety of pedagogical activities (which we discuss throughout the book) that give students an active role in shaping their own learning and redistribute power from the teacher to students (so that they can develop as learners) (Weimer, 2013). Learner-centered activities are personalized, addressing the specific needs, goals, and/or backgrounds of the student population, and students are encouraged to make choices about their learning. For example, students may have the option to select some readings, choose among possible assignments, establish the parameters for course policies, and more. Learner-centered activities foster students' development as expert learners and also increase their motivation.

Learner-centered activities are also frequently collaborative, or require students to work together in some way. Weimer (2013) synthesizes research on the effectiveness of having students work in well-designed group activities. Research suggests that when students work together, they have to explain concepts to one another and this articulation deepens their learning. Weimer (2013) also reports that multiple studies have demonstrated that active, learner-centered approaches significantly improve students' satisfaction with the course, including their interest, learning, and evaluation of the instructor (p. 48).

Alignment and Learning Outcomes for Effective Course Design

When designing courses, most people have had little or no training in how to do so effectively. Faculty may start with texts they plan to use or ideas for activities or a list of important topics to cover. *Backward design* (Wiggins & McTighe, 2005) instead asks us to begin with what we want students to know and be able to do at the end of the course and with the essential questions the course is going to pursue. Essential questions are a way of reframing course goals to focus the course more effectively. For example:

- To what extent does art reflect culture or shape it?
- Must a story have a beginning, a middle, and an end?
- Is everything quantifiable? (Wiggins & McTighe, 2005)

Essential questions are broad, compelling, and often cut across disciplinary boundaries and/or define fields. They "stimulate thought [...] provoke inquiry [...] and spark more questions" (Wiggins & McTighe, 2005). They keep the focus on big ideas.

Table 4.1 Sample Learning Outcomes

Knowledge	Students will be able to...
	• examine the development of Concept X over time and across cultures;
	• articulate how a system, trend, or issue is interrelated with others;
	• analyze an issue from multiple perspectives using input from diverse people; and
	• describe the values that three different cultures take toward X.
Skills	Students will be able to...
	• communicate effectively with diverse peoples to complete Project X; and
	• identify credible sources of information about Diverse Group X.
Attitudes	Students will be willing to...
	• engage in intercultural problem-solving with diverse peoples;
	• accept that diverse peoples have differing concepts of what is logical or natural; and
	• value the different linguistic resources that members bring to the group.

With essential questions driving the design of the course, the next step is to determine what students will be able to achieve at the end of the course. Learning outcomes are then the results of the course—a one-sentence description of what students should know, value, or be able to do upon completion. Strong learning outcomes should be written from the student's perspective in clear language. Outcomes should address a variety of Bloom's (1956) taxonomy levels and should be both measurable and observable.

Table 4.1 provides broad examples of learning outcomes that include a global perspective. One could further strengthen these outcomes by personalizing them with a time frame (e.g., "By the end of this project") and by specifying the activity through which faculty will assess whether the outcome has been achieved (e.g., "through class discussion" or "in Project X").

Classroom Strategies and *The Workshop* offer ways to modify existing outcomes to include a global and inclusive perspective by considering the knowledge, skills, and attitudes students need.

Once strong learning outcomes have been developed, then Wiggins and McTighe (2005) suggest faculty establish how they will know that those outcomes have been achieved. What assignments and activities will students need to complete to show what they've learned? After faculty have established the foundations for the course, they are now ready to choose readings and plan daily activities. Thus, backward design is a procedure:

1. What are the essential questions this course investigates?
2. What do students need to know, value, and be able to do by the end?
3. How will students demonstrate what they know, value, and are able to do?
4. What texts, activities, and experiences will prepare students to demonstrate this?

This procedure ensures that faculty have defined what students will learn (as opposed to choosing a list of topics) and have *alignment* between those learnings, how students will be assessed, and the class's daily activities.

Universal Design for Learning

Universal Design for Learning, or UDL, is a relatively new pedagogy that focuses on making learning accessible to a more diverse array of students and helping all learners to become expert learners. UDL works in contrast to traditional approaches that were designed for one "model" or "average" learner. Developed in response to neuroscience on human variability, UDL uses that variability as a baseline, asking instructors to focus on the learning goal or outcome while allowing students to meet it in multiple ways. Meyer, Rose, and Gordon (2014, p. 82) point out the difficulties that categories can produce in our classrooms:

> One of the most important revelations emerging from brain research is that the notion of broad categories of learners – smart/not smart, disabled/not disabled, regular/not regular – is a gross over-simplification that does not reflect reality. By categorizing people this way, we place an undue burden on individuals to adapt themselves in all their wonderful diversity to inflexible learning environments [...]. [O]ur learning environments [should] be designed with a deep understanding and appreciation for individual variability.

It is because of this emphasis on variability as strength that we discuss UDL here. It supports diverse learners in substantive ways and, thus, is well suited to our goal of fostering a global perspective.

The three main principles of UDL are:

- Provide multiple means of engagement (the "why" of learning).
- Provide multiple means of representation (the "what" of learning).
- Provide multiple means of action and expression (the "how" of learning) (Meyer et al., 2014, p. 89).

Providing multiple means of engagement challenges instructors to help learners develop resilience and coping skills as well as to get learners interested and engaged by letting them work in contexts that are authentic and valuable *to them*. Meyer et al. (2014, p. 91) write that:

> It is critically important to design learning contexts that offer flexibility in the domain of engagement so that each student can find a way into the learning experience, remain persistent in the face of challenge or failure, and continue to build self-knowledge.

The second principle, "provide multiple means of representation" (Meyer et al., 2014, p. 99), encourages faculty to communicate information to learners in a variety of ways. Faculty might work to make sure that important background information is available for learners and to present information in a variety of ways, for example through both video and in print, so that learners have multiple ways to access the information and may do so repeatedly if needed. "When content is represented through two or more mediums of text, image, video, or audio, learners' strengths and interests in all of these media become potential avenues for success and engagement" (Meyer et al., 2014, p. 102).

Finally, "provide multiple means for action and expression" (Meyer et al., 2014, p. 111) asks faculty to allow students to demonstrate their knowledge in a range of ways while also helping students learn how to set and achieve goals. For instance, students might have the option to write a paper *or* give a presentation *or* create a video instead of requiring everyone to write a paper. Instead of a timed, in-class exam, students might work out of class where they can utilize voice-to-text software or have additional time to research a topic that is more interesting to them.

 ## CLASSROOM STRATEGIES

"How can I make my courses more active and learner-centered?"

Many instructors are moving away from traditional lecture-based course structures into formats that allow for more student interaction and self-direction and that also challenge students to apply their knowledge. There are many possibilities for making classes more active, including adding discussion, think-pair-shares (where students first respond to a problem individually, then discuss with a partner before sharing with the class), projects, presentations, writing projects, and more (see Chapter 6). There are also a plethora of technology-based options like assessing students' knowledge through polling software, allowing them to ask questions or comment on each other's work using social media, or having them work together in online spaces like blogs, wikis, etc. We discuss many of these active, learner-centered methods throughout the book.

In recent years, there's also been a movement toward complete course format changes like flipped classrooms, team-based learning, problem-based learning, and online or blended instruction. Each has its own benefits as well as challenges for diverse student populations. A significant discussion of these options is beyond our scope here, but we have suggested some starting points in the bibliography. We encourage you to contact your university's instructional designer or teaching center for further support.

In the *Case Study* below, Ashley Metcalf describes how she redesigned her course to include global perspectives and to vary the course format in order to increase student engagement.

CASE STUDY: TEACHING FROM A GLOBAL PERSPECTIVE—COURSE REDESIGN

I teach an undergraduate course in Operations Management which is required for all Business students. This course covers the basics of project management, process design/management, and global supply chains. Historically, this class has been taught from a very traditional lecture and exams format. I have been thinking of ways to redesign the course, and even introduced an online simulation to try to get students engaged. But, the online simulation was not enough. Lectures were still the main method of teaching and I knew I needed more student engagement.

Since I have many international students in my course every semester, I started thinking about how I could better incorporate global perspectives into the curriculum and also enhance student engagement. I started with my syllabus and materials. I made sure course objectives specifically stated global and international perspectives. In addition, I changed course materials (readings/handouts/videos) to also include global examples, like using case studies involving companies located in another country. Also, I gave examples of US companies dealing with global issues (logistics, ethics, culture, language, etc.) during their out-sourcing or expansion initiatives.

Next, I worked to change the traditional format to something more engaging. Now I start class with a recent news article or video related to the day's topic. Then, I do a short lecture that leads to a point of discussion. I break students into teams and let them discuss the topics in small groups. Students are able to reach conclusions and identify problems that relate directly to the topic of the day. After a short debrief by each group, we go over example problems and any related calculations. So, even though I don't cover as much in my lecture materials, I feel like the major issues/topics are still being discussed in each class and students are much more engaged and collaborative with their classmates.

Dr. Ashley Metcalf
Assistant Professor of Operations Management
Ohio University

Ashley Metcalf's course redesign allowed her to not only help students build their global perspective, but also hold classes that are more engaging and interactive for her undergraduates.

"How can I implement Universal Design for Learning (UDL) into my courses?"

Many of the activities in this book aim to shift faculty toward practices that are consistent with UDL. A few specific ideas are given below.

- Develop multiple ways to give students information; the syllabus (which we discuss below) is one example. If students receive a traditional syllabus and a just-the-highlights graphic syllabus in addition to hearing about the syllabus in class, then they're much more likely to comprehend it.
- Build an "Other" option into every assignment. If the goals of the assignment can still be met, then allow students to make a case to do another version of the assignment that will be more interesting and useful to them. If the goals of the assignment *can't* be met, then look for ways to compromise and meet some of everyone's goals.
- When the goal of an assignment is to demonstrate what students have learned, allow them to do so through a variety of modes (e.g., a presentation, a paper, or a video) instead of prescribing the mode (e.g., "write a final paper"). This flexibility allows students to demonstrate their knowledge in the mode where they are most comfortable, fluent, and talented.

Sherri Saines, Ohio University librarian, suggests these ways of meeting learning outcomes for research with secondary sources without assigning a research paper:

- Write out learning objectives for research. If the objective is to learn to read an article, *give* them an article and analyze it together in class. If the objective, on the other hand, is to *find* articles, ask your librarian to teach students how to manipulate database searches for efficiency.
- Assign students a challenging but short reading—the more outlandish the better. Work together to examine each fact, proving its truth or falsehood with outside sources. Create a table: fact from article vs. fact from another source and its citation.
- Ask students to gather and transcribe an oral history story from someone older to open doors of communication across generations and cultures. Next, have them find a similar, published story and compare the two.
- Give students an essential paper in the field and work through it in class. Have your librarian teach students how to track its use over time. Each student discovers something very current that cites it and explains its relationship to the original paper, expanding comprehension without requiring an extended research project.

"What are global learning outcomes (GLOs)?"

Courses with learning outcomes that promote a global mindset and inclusivity ask students to develop the knowledge, skills, and attitudes needed to engage with other cultures. As they do so, GLOs simultaneously demonstrate to students that diverse perspectives and communication patterns are valued. Like any strong learning outcome, GLOs need to be aligned with course content and be measurable and observable. They also need to ask students to develop or demonstrate a global perspective.

Faculty in the humanities or social sciences often find it straightforward to implement GLOs, while in STEM courses, GLOs might ask students from diverse backgrounds to interact and learn from each other, for instructors (including international teaching assistants) and students to communicate authentically, and for students to develop an identity as a member of the scientific community. In some cases, existing learning outcomes can be broadened to encourage a global perspective, while in others a more in-depth revision of outcomes may be necessary. In Table 4.2 below, we've modified a variety of outcomes to include a global perspective.

Including at least some GLOs that encourage students to develop a global perspective and enable diverse students to feel included in course content is an important step in developing a global perspective.

Table 4.2 Creating Global Learning Outcomes

Original Learning Outcome	Revised Global Learning Outcome
Students will be able to...	
Engage in research about the politics of food production.	Engage in research about the politics of food production in both local and global contexts.
Demonstrate critical thinking and reading skills.	Demonstrate critical thinking and reading skills in multiple cultural contexts.
Generate a hypothesis from a set of observations and then suggest experiments to test the hypothesis.	Generate a hypothesis from a set of observations and then suggest experiments to test the hypothesis, utilizing data sources from diverse groups.
Define factors in the spread of infectious diseases.	Define factors in the spread of infectious diseases, including at least three distinct global regions and how local behaviors and perspectives affect transmission.
Demonstrate understanding of the process of converting raw materials to commercial products by constructing and analyzing flow diagrams.	Demonstrate understanding of the process of converting raw materials to commercial products by constructing and analyzing flow diagrams in two distinct global contexts; compare processes and results.
Work with classmates on new material in class (involves teamwork, communicating in mathematics and frequent, careful checking of answers).	Work with classmates from diverse backgrounds on new material in class (involves teamwork, communicating about mathematics across cultures, and frequent, careful checking of answers).
Develop the skills necessary to work collaboratively in order to be contributing members to the course project.	Develop the interpersonal skills necessary to work collaboratively and effectively with others in order to be contributing members in a global society.

"How can I design more effective assignments?"

Strong assignments share several essential features. First, they are aligned to meet learning outcomes, or they create situations in which students' work will demonstrate a learning outcome of the course. As they meet those outcomes, strong assignments clearly articulate their purpose to students. They also clearly identify the components required, timeframe, and grading criteria. An assignment that encourages a global perspective builds on this foundation by:

- encouraging active and goal-oriented learning,
- encouraging critical thinking about another context or culture, and
- requiring interaction with a population different from the student's own.

While innovative assignments offer students the opportunity for increased and more personalized learning, some students, particularly those who have studied in other contexts, may find this innovation challenging. If your assignments ask students to choose their own topics, consider scaffolding students through this learning process. For example, a presentation assignment might be broken down into three smaller assignments. Students might begin by submitting a statement of the topic and focus area. Next, they might bring an outline of main points with references to an individual conference with the instructor or to receive feedback from classmates. Once students have developed an appropriate topic and received feedback on their main ideas, they are much better prepared to give the final presentation. While using this kind of step-by-step scaffolding does take instructor time, many find that overall time is reduced since students' final work is stronger, reducing the time needed for grading. Scaffolding also allows faculty to identify and resolve confusion before large difficulties occur (see Chapter 6). In the Case Study below, Mick Andzulis shares how he revised a major assignment to scaffold it more effectively and to incorporate a global perspective.

CASE STUDY: SETTING STUDENTS UP FOR SUCCESS

I teach a new Sales Strategy & Technology class and quickly realized that I could be both more strategic and intentional in how I support my undergraduates as they develop a more global perspective. One change I've made is to incorporate scaffolding to my assignments. I also challenge students to provide meaningful feedback to each other. In the "Salesperson Interview Assignment" I wanted to expand the students' learning experience, so I first created in-class workshops and student feedback sessions to develop, prepare, and refine questions that students could use in their interviews. I also decided to highlight a global element by encouraging students to collaborate with someone from a different background, or to interview professionals from other countries, even conducting the interview in a language other than English.

In my revised course, I share feedback with students in class and offer the opportunity for revisions and even extra credit for students or groups that choose to present their findings to the class so that we can all learn from each student's experience. I have tried informal sharing sessions before, but now I'm more structured in how I design these assignments and share times in order to elicit greater learning and more participation from students. For example, I now ask students to share any excellent interview questions their partners developed, and we then discuss them as a class, which enables each student to improve her or his own strategy for the interview assignment. My students like these assignments and are now pushing themselves to be more global in their thinking.

Dr. Mick Andzulis
Assistant Professor of Marketing
Ohio University

"In what areas might students need extra support?"

Depending on their previous educational experiences, some students may have unique needs related to their awareness of common US academic and social expectations. For instance, compared with the rest of the world, US classrooms are less hierarchical, resulting in less formal relationships between faculty and students. In many countries, it is not uncommon for a course to not have a detailed syllabus with learning outcomes, assignments, weightings, and a course schedule. These differences can lead to confusion and discomfort for students used to a different academic culture. Students may not be aware of their rights, appeal processes, or various academic expectations. Below are some specific areas where students with different educational experiences may benefit from explicit discussion of your expectations, as well as a *Case Study* from a research librarian describing a method for providing extra support during research projects.

1. Higher-Order Critical Thinking Skills and Active Learning

Many cultures emphasize memorization over critical thinking skills, with teachers and materials (e.g., textbooks) regarded as unquestionable authorities. Students from these cultures may perceive asking questions as a sign of disrespect. They may also struggle with developing their own learning goals and evaluating and synthesizing sources. In other cases, high-stakes testing cultures have strongly conditioned students to expect the "one right answer." These students often struggle when asked to engage in critical, nuanced thinking and have difficulty coping when a problem has multiple valuable answers or a range of answers, all of which are somehow limited.

2. Participation, Peer Collaboration, and Group Work

Many cultures emphasize individual academic achievement over peer collaboration, which can lead to competition between classmates. Some of these students will then question the value of collaboration and the very idea of learning from peers instead of the teacher. Others will struggle with ambiguities inherent in grading group projects and in participation expectations (see also Chapter 5).

3. Approaching the Teacher with a Problem or Question

In many cultures, students are not encouraged to approach faculty and the practice of office hours doesn't exist. This is often due to large class sizes. Students may turn to classmates over the instructor with questions and may need several invitations to come to office hours. When students do approach faculty, they may state questions or concerns indirectly, necessitating extra attention and questioning from instructors.

CASE STUDY: HELPING STUDENTS FIND AND EVALUATE SOURCES

I am a librarian, and I collaborate with faculty frequently to improve student learning about information. As often happens, the faculty member I was working with that day was frustrated because her students weren't effectively synthesizing information into their research projects. They could find things that looked relevant, but they couldn't discern how applicable those articles really were, nor show they had digested the ideas, or come to creative conclusions. This was even more marked among international students, which was surprising as they had shown multiple times that they could understand the academic literature she assigned. Yet some students come from places without databases, large libraries, or reliable internet. Many other countries' information architectures still rely very heavily on print monographs and the whole concept of academic articles may be unfamiliar. Collaborating with your subject librarian to devise assignments and class exercises that meet your information learning objectives can have a positive impact on student success.

Collaborating with the faculty member, we addressed students' problems by first closely analyzing the assignment and its assumptions.

I was able to add to her understanding because of what I know about libraries and research in other countries and suggest some changes.

For example, because most international students do not know they can ask a librarian for help, we added a classroom visit by the subject librarian. During that visit, the librarian took pains to cover some differences between libraries in other countries and those on US college campuses, such as the ability to check out unlimited numbers of books, overnight study spaces, group study spaces, reserve readings, and the fact that your library record is not archived and cannot be traced back to you.

To address the applicability problem, we built an extra in-class assignment. They worked together to search a database, tracking the words they used and the number and kind of results on the list. Next, they chose one article that seemed to be on the topic. By opening the abstract, and then the full text of the article itself, they could analyze whether this was in fact applicable, or just a "false drop" (i.e., all the individual search terms appeared in the article description, but not the concepts those words create together). Concentrating on one article's applicability seemed to drive the point home that students would have to look beyond the title to find relevant articles.

We also instituted an exercise in gathering vocabulary for better database searching—a special challenge if your first language is not English. In this exercise, they created a logically structured list of words for each concept in the topic. While searching, they first looked for and collected related terms and synonyms for each concept. With this list in hand, I demonstrated using *and* and *or* to broaden or limit results. This list is useful for every subsequent search in other databases, and the list continues to grow as students master their topic.

After incorporating these changes, students demonstrated better results the next semester. We have continued to collaborate to tweak and improve student success on her assignment.

Sherri Saines
Social Sciences Subject Librarian
Ohio University

"How can I encourage students to come to office hours?"

Some students benefit from one-on-one support but are apprehensive about coming to office hours, for example due to shyness or cultural differences. Try:

- providing positive reinforcement when students do come;
- giving students challenging problems to solve so they need individualized help;
- providing feedback on assignments or help sessions during (required) office hours;
- having students collect something from your office (e.g., a handout, a graded assignment) so that they are encouraged to make future visits; and
- meeting in a public space, with the door open, and/or with colleagues nearby if you are concerned about impropriety or safety.

"How can I get students to read the syllabus?"

Helping students to understand, remember, and carry out their obligations in the syllabus is certainly challenging. Try:

- creating an alternative syllabus that is more focused on students' common questions. Instead of (or to supplement) a traditional syllabus, design a one- or two-page graphic syllabus that showcases your most important policies and briefly describes assignments. A quick web search will offer many examples;
- creating a quiz around students' most common mistakes. Allow students to take the quiz as many times as needed to learn key policies;
- recording a short video or making an FAQ that highlights solutions to common questions;
- providing each student with one or two "passes" that they can use as automatic extensions on assignments or absolution for not preparing for class. The passes acknowledge that we all have tough days and make mistakes while minimizing requests for exceptions.

 THE WORKSHOP

4.1 Unpacking Our Curricula

This workshop leads you through a systematic examination of your curriculum to consider how it might be made more global and inclusive. Note that it's certainly helpful to partner with a colleague to counteract each other's blind spots. Another possibility is that your multicultural, LGBTQ, or teaching center *might* help faculty with this kind of work. We offer this vital caveat though: *It is not the responsibility of your diverse colleagues to teach you how to make your courses more diverse and inclusive.* Diverse colleagues are often asked to engage in additional, unpaid labor in order to make curricula, programs, professions, etc., more inclusive. This unpaid labor is an important equity issue for diverse colleagues who should be compensated and recognized for making these contributions. Consider working through the following steps in order to diversify your coursework or curricula:

1. Examine your formal curriculum (syllabi, assignments, assessments, etc.) and identify the values and cultures you are promoting (i.e., your hidden curriculum). What other values are you potentially excluding? What problematic assumptions might the formal curriculum lead students to make? Example: While examining her Introduction to Business syllabus, Professor Jennifer realizes that much of her material and discussion points include cultural references and vocabulary that may not be understood by international students. And, while some case studies are international, they have embedded American values that aren't transparent. She also notices that some students may not have any experience with free enterprise systems, thereby limiting contributions they can make to class. Finally, she sees that some students lack the vocabulary to discuss topics related to ethical tensions in business.

2. Examine these same materials from a global perspective. What materials, activities, or assignments give students an opportunity to share their own cultures? What materials, activities, and assignments help students to cultivate a global perspective or assess the development of a global perspective?

3. What changes could you make to materials, activities, and assignments to encourage students' development of a global perspective?

4. Examine regular extracurricular opportunities at your institution and community (i.e., the informal curriculum). In what ways do these activities promote or discourage students' critical thinking about their own and others' cultures?

5. Within your sphere of influence, how could you change the informal curriculum to better support students' development of a global perspective? Could you invite diverse speakers to colloquia? Develop a new film series that spotlights diverse voices? Relocate a field trip so that it introduces students to a different culture? Highlight existing diverse activities on your campus for your students?

4.2 Assessing Course Learning Outcomes for a Global Perspective

Analyze how your course outcomes encourage students to approach content and communication with a global perspective and then revise accordingly. You can access the AAC&U's Global Learning VALUE Rubric at www.aacu.org/value/rubrics/global-learning in order to assess how well your course supports global learning for your students.

Original Learning Outcome	Revised Global Learning Outcome
Students will be able to...	
1.	
2.	
3.	

4.3 Unpacking your Department's Curricula

Now that you've analyzed your courses for their global perspective, apply what you've learned to your program as a whole. We encourage you to complete this workshop with your colleagues, for example as a project of your department's curriculum or retention committee.

1. Brainstorm the knowledge, skills, and attitudes your students need in order to succeed in the field and/or be global thinkers and communicators.
2. Collect your department's formal curriculum (e.g., syllabi from required courses, course and programmatic assessments) and identify the values and cultures your department is promoting (i.e., your hidden curriculum). What other values are you potentially excluding? What problematic assumptions might the formal curriculum lead students to make?
3. In which courses do the learning outcomes and assignments ask students to demonstrate a global perspective? Are enough courses engaged in this work? Could courses be revised to do this work more effectively?
4. Is there an opportunity to develop a new course with the specific goal of increasing students' global perspective? What would that course look like?
5. Examine your department's extracurricular opportunities. How do these activities promote or discourage students from thinking critically about their own and others' cultures? Could they do more to foster a global perspective?
6. Take a Cultures and Values Walk through your department, both physically and digitally. Are the entrances accessible? What is on the walls? On the website? What do your findings say about your department's values? How

could you be more inclusive? Obviously, it is easier to change a website than to re-engineer an inaccessible entrance, yet what changes do you have the power to make, even if they can't completely eliminate a problem?

 DISCUSSION AND REFLECTION

1. What is missing in extracurricular activities (the informal curriculum) on your campus that would make a difference to students you know? Who can or should make those changes happen?
2. What are your preferred teaching activities? Are the active- and learner-centered approaches described here typical for your classes? What new activities might you try?
3. The *Case Studies* by both Ashley Metcalf and Mick Andzulis describe how they redeveloped assignments so that more global perspectives were included. Now that you've analyzed your own curricula, what ideas do you have for strengthening the global perspective in your courses?
4. While in some teaching contexts there may be an even distribution of diverse students, often courses have just a few students from different backgrounds. This situation can be more challenging for the instructor and the student(s) who may feel left out. How can UDL help you strategize for this situation as you plan learning experiences?

 BIBLIOGRAPHY

Acker, S. (2001). The hidden curriculum of dissertation advising. In E. Margolis (Ed.), *The hidden curriculum in higher education*. New York, NY: Routledge.

Ambrose, S., Bridges, M., DiPietro, M., Lovett, M., & Norman, M. (2010). *How learning works: 7 research-based principles for smart teaching*. San Francisco, CA: Jossey-Bass.

Bean, J. (2011). *Engaging ideas: The professor's guide to integrating writing, critical thinking, and active learning in the classroom* (2nd ed.). San Francisco, CA: Jossey-Bass.

Bloom, B. (1956). *Taxonomy of educational objectives, Handbook I: The cognitive domain*. New York: David McKay.

Herman, J., & Nilson, L. (2018). *Creating engaging discussions: Strategies for "avoiding crickets" in any size classroom and online*. Sterling, VA: Stylus.

Killick, D. (2015). *Developing the global student: Higher education in an era of globalization*. London, UK: Routledge.

Linder, K. (2016). *The blended course design workbook: A practical guide*. Sterling, VA: Stylus.

Meyer, A., Rose, D., & Gordon, D. (2014). *Universal design for learning: Theory and practice.* Wakefield, MA: CAST Professional Publishing.

Michaelsen, L., Knight, A., & Fink, L. (2002). *Team-based learning: A transformative use of small groups.* Westport, CT: Praeger.

Prince, M. (2004). Does active learning work? A review of the research. *Journal of Engineering Education, 93*(3), 223–231.

Sambell, K., & McDowell, L. (1998). The construction of the hidden curriculum: Messages and meanings in the assessment of student learning. *Assessment and Evaluation in Higher Education, 23*(4), 391–402.

Weimer, M. (2013). *Learner-centered teaching: five key changes to practice* (2nd ed.). New York, NY: Wiley.

Wiggins, G., & McTighe, J. (2005). *Understanding by design* (2nd ed.). Upper Saddle River, NJ: Pearson Education.

Chapter 5

Designing for Participation in the Global Classroom

 INTRODUCTION

In this chapter, we examine participation and how faculty can structure class time in order to maximize opportunities for students to more fully engage with different groups and consequently expand their global mindset and learning. A sense of connection for students translates into greater participation, smoother communication, and, when applicable, stronger teams or groups. This connection requires interaction, both academically and socially, since "learning involves the whole person" and occurs in social contexts, particularly for deeper learning to occur (Lave & Wenger, 1998, p. 53). Integration between all types of students allows them to take advantage of the benefits that internationalization can offer (Andrade, 2006) and can lead to higher academic performance, for example for international students (Glass, 2012). Ensuring that all students feel that they are on the same footing, or are communicating as "true peers" (Killick, 2015, p. 160), is thus crucial in the global classroom. The goal is to help students feel comfortable while also pushing them to think critically and grow both intellectually and emotionally. Acknowledging that many faculty already feel pressured to cram too much academic material into too little time, this chapter explores concepts related to supporting participation across the segments of your student population, focusing on strategies that build engagement.

By the end of this chapter, you should be able to:

- discuss the role of engagement and connection in students' participation in a global classroom;
- identify and discuss challenges that students may experience as they work to participate in a global classroom;

- identify and discuss challenges that faculty face in facilitating participation during class and for out-of-class assignments; and
- identify strategies to increase students' participation in class, particularly those students who may not be comfortable or accustomed to doing so.

CLASSROOM AND SELF-ASSESSMENT

Before reading *Key Concepts* and identifying specific strategies you can use in your context, take a moment to reflect on your situation by rating your students' in-class engagement and participation. Note how your students rank and if their perspective seems to develop over time. For ideas on how to go about assessing students' knowledge and values, see the Preface. We also ask you to assess to what degree your classes provide an environment that best facilitates participation and engagement.

ASSESSING HOW YOUR STUDENTS ENGAGE AND PARTICIPATE DURING CLASS

Student engagement with the material and each other builds opportunities for peer learning, particularly regarding issues related to a global education. To what degree do your students demonstrate the ability and willingness to participate in class in terms of their communication behaviors, their listening skills, and their knowledge of cultural norms and expectations? Are there opportunities to increase student engagement in class that you might be missing?

By the time students leave my class/department, they:

0	actively avoid participating in class discussions, asking questions, talking with classmates, or listening to lectures.
☆	occasionally engage in class through discussions or interacting with classmates from different backgrounds, but interaction is limited and superficial and comments do not reflect a respect for others' opinions or backgrounds.
☆ ☆	engage in class discussions, but mainly the same few students and comments may not reflect critical thinking or cultural awareness; demonstrate strong interest in working with classmates from different backgrounds, but are unsure of how to build new knowledge from class discussions or group work and unsure of how to include all perspectives.
☆ ☆ ☆	actively engage in class, with nearly all students participating in discussions, listening to diverse perspectives, building new understandings from each other, and supporting each other's learning.

ASSESSING WHETHER YOU ARE STRUCTURING A CLASS ENVIRONMENT THAT ENCOURAGES ENGAGEMENT AND PARTICIPATION

The way we structure our classrooms is a reflection of our own assumptions about learning and teaching. Where does motivation stem from, in your mind, and what is the role of the instructor in facilitating student engagement?

In my own teaching, I:

☆	value student responsibility and do not feel a professor can do much to influence student motivation; students should come to class motivated so that I can help them meet their goals.
☆ ☆	value active learning and would like to structure classes that are more engaging, such as with more participation in discussions or more flow of communication across groups of students, but I am unsure of how to accomplish this.
☆ ☆ ☆	have prioritized student engagement in my classes through how I structure in-class activities; I assess student engagement through various means, including bringing in outside perspectives or student voices, and make modifications as needed; I receive course evaluation comments indicating a strong environment for active learning.

Example of a faculty member moving from a two- to three-star level in structuring their class environment to maximize participation: A College of Business faculty member who wants to increase reflection and participation reorders her in-class time. Instead of lecturing on key points after showing a video, she now groups students and asks them to discuss and identify how video content relates to class goals. She chooses videos and asks questions that students from various backgrounds can likely relate to and monitors discussions for involvement and respect.

The remaining sections in this chapter provide background information on ways to structure class time that will maximize student engagement and participation.

KEY CONCEPTS

Course design is the first step in planning for participation, but for many instructors, it is the facilitation of in-class interaction that is more challenging. Participation is a term often used but rarely defined. Most use the term to refer to students raising their hands and offering comments or questions during group discussions, but other behaviors can also be included, such as short conversations between classmates or between students and instructors, pair or group work, or even oral presentations. Some students even view participation as doing their homework, being prepared for class, and listening carefully (Fritschner, 2000) (i.e., "silent participation" Meyer, 2009, p. 131). Participation can vary not only depending on the course and its level (upper vs. lower), but also based on students' gender, age, background (Fritschner, 2000), and personality type.

While many instructors include participation grades in their syllabi, research has shown that these grades do not necessarily lead to increased participation among all students; a greater role may be played by students' own learning style and strategy preferences. Students who believe that their learning is facilitated by oral in-class participation and who believe they have an ethical responsibility to speak in class are more likely to participate than those who do not feel that speaking in class benefits them or that they are bound ethically to share their opinions (Meyer, 2009). Faculty may thus want to focus more on students' overall engagement with the course and peers, demonstrating to students how participation can positively impact their learning, as they utilize a definition of participation that matches the learning goals of their own contexts and student populations. Student participation can also be affected by classroom dynamics; minority students, females, first-generation college students, and non-native English speakers may be less likely to participate than white males (Hall & Sandler, 1982; Yaylacı & Beauvais, 2017). These findings have implications for classrooms working to help students develop a global perspective; we need to hear the diverse views in our courses, yet we acknowledge that students' silence in class does not necessarily indicate a lack of engagement.

Engagement and Connection in a Global Classroom

Regardless of the specific definition used for participation, what faculty are seeking is for students to engage with the material. Engagement can be seen as students putting forth extra "effort and involvement in productive learning activities" (Kuh, 2009, p. 6). In other words, in-class participation is much more meaningful when the people in the room (physical or virtual) connect. For some students, interactions in class are particularly important for social contact and academic success (e.g., see Stoynoff, 1997).

Connection can be difficult when classmates and/or faculty hold diverse views or come from diverse backgrounds: "The ultimate challenge facing any [...] global citizen, is not merely to communicate, but to *connect*" (Gerzon, 2010, p. 87). Gerzon (2010) emphasizes the importance of trust: "The challenge of connecting is to build a bridge of trust across a divide in order that the two or

103

more individuals or groups can work together more effectively" (p. 87) and "break out of the straightjacket of a single identity" (p. 90). Building on this trust, learning is possible when students are able to interact with each other and ask questions "that open up new possibilities"; notice the complexity in people's multiple identities; and truly listen even when they disagree (Gerzon, p. 91). It takes careful planning to structure and facilitate classroom experiences that support communication as well as students' development as global citizens.

Course planning is illustrated in the following *Case Study*, in which a faculty member reflects on her experiences as an international student trying to engage in class and how those experiences have shaped how she approaches her own teaching.

CASE STUDY: ENCOURAGING PARTICIPATION IN CLASS

In a college English literature class of about fifty students, our professor decided one day to randomly call on students from the class roster. Until then, only two or three students had dared to make comments or ask questions. I appreciated this class very much, but this particular day, as he called my name and followed up with a question, I wished I had not been there because I could only understand half of what he was saying. Being an international student from Chile, I was fairly fluent in English, but his question contained a word or two that I did not know and admitting this publicly did not seem like a viable option. The professor said my name a couple of times more, but since nobody reacted, he assumed that I was absent and called on another student. The best solution I could come up with was to pretend not to be there. Fortunately, in a lecture class my "silent reply" had worked.

By now I sit (or rather stand) on the other side. As an instructor of Spanish language and Spanish American literature, I cannot help thinking that often times my students feel exactly the same way I felt that day. Even as I gain teaching experience, I try to remember my own process of learning English and other foreign languages. While calling on names is usually an effective tactic to encourage participation, in my experience it tends to work better in some class contexts than others. In more advanced language or literature courses, I set up small-group discussions and after circulating between these groups, I take the chance to invite some of the quieter students to rearticulate and share their observations with the rest of the class. Another tactic I have found useful for engaging shyer students is asking them to read a passage aloud from a text. Sometimes just having their voice resound in the classroom is enough of an invitation for them to participate next time voluntarily. A final strategy is having students record a short audio clip (between 30–45 seconds) based on an assigned reading before the class meets. This assignment holds students accountable for the reading, gives me a preliminary idea of each student's comprehension (which in turn helps me finalize my preparation to lead class discussions), and provides me the chance to hear all of their voices in Spanish.

In the end, when it comes to encouraging participation I think it is important to take into account that understanding and speaking a foreign language requires not only constant effort from the student, but also from the instructor. It is crucial to give all students more than one chance to participate in class and to do this in various ways, especially before they resort to pretending they are not really present in the classroom.

Dr. Paula Park
Assistant Professor of Spanish
Wesleyan University

Paula Park's *Case Study* shares how she has maintained her expectations for class participation, yet also developed support systems and activities for students who may be more shy or hesitant to speak in class. While she focuses on a language classroom, her strategies can apply to many other contexts as well and highlight some of the challenges inherent in helping students participate in global learning environments.

Challenges to Participation in the Global Classroom

Simply placing students who hold different beliefs or are from different backgrounds together in a group, or leading large-class discussions, will not automatically lead to successful participation in a global classroom. Some of the challenges lie in the affective realm. Some students worry about talking too much and frustrating classmates (Fritschner, 2000, p. 352), while others struggle with low self-confidence or fears of receiving negative feedback from their professors (Meyer, 2009). International students may feel that their domestic peers dominate class discussions (Tatar, 2005), while domestic students may feel that peers from other countries are unnecessarily reticent. Social tensions can arise in diverse groups and affect communication as well (Takahashi & Saito, 2013). Many students are unaware of how their behavior may affect classmates' perceptions of belonging or a willingness to share ideas. They may also be unaware of the ideas and perspectives that other viewpoints can offer. Gender can play a role in participation as well: students from some backgrounds or countries (e.g., Saudi Arabia) may be uncomfortable working in gender-mixed groups, while this interaction is expected by other students; faculty may struggle to ensure a gender balance during class discussions (Hall & Sandler, 1982; Yaylacı & Beauvais, 2017). In online communication, students may post disrespectful comments, choose not to engage with peers different from themselves, or simply drop the course if they feel offended or unheard.

Challenges also lie in expectations. A faculty expectation in this area that may differ from student expectations is in the use of technology in the classroom, with some faculty feeling that devices or laptops distract students from discussions and real-time interactions, and students valuing their technology use in class. Students have conflicting expectations as well, such as different expectations about how to accomplish a collaborative activity or how they will be assessed. They may distrust collaborative pedagogies, based on previous frustrations and experiences, and may prefer to work on their own. They may lack a shared understanding about each other's backgrounds or communication expectations, which can affect interaction (Fozdar & Volet, 2012). Groups of native English-speaking students and multilingual students can lead to frustration related to expectations regarding language proficiency (Moore & Hampton, 2015). Even students who are interested in engaging in groups with peers different from themselves find it quite challenging (Fozdar & Volet, 2012). Other students may come from educational experiences that have no expectation of speaking in class or who are accustomed to waiting their turn before sharing an opinion.

Barriers to participation relate to content as well. Students who are unable to follow the material or lectures will struggle to join fast-paced discussions. Using examples or cases that students cannot connect with their lives presents an obstacle to understanding. Relying on examples or discussion question topics related to the mainstream culture, for example, can exclude some students from a conversation. The following *Case Study* illustrates challenges in student participation, showcasing a student who faced the types of difficulties discussed above and then developed his own plan for how to get the most from group work. As faculty, we can look for opportunities to support students as they develop their own strategies as well.

CASE STUDY: HELPING STUDENTS OVERCOME GROUP WORK CHALLENGES

As part of my research (Phillips, 2008), I did a case study with an international graduate student named Chozin. In his first semester, he was in a mixed undergraduate/graduate class and had to complete a large group assignment as part of his final grade. Research has shown pretty consistently that group projects are especially difficult for international, multilingual students. They may not have the pragmatic competence to participate effectively, they may not have the language skills to participate effectively, and their native English-speaking peers may view them as a liability as a result. In Chozin's case, he also had no knowledge of the topic area for the project. The rest of the group—Ohio undergraduates—chose to study something in the nearby city of Cincinnati; Chozin had no knowledge of Cincinnati or of the local topic that the group was studying. He had a very bad experience in the group and was often excluded from meetings; his peers wouldn't even respond to his requests for meeting dates and locations. Chozin was frustrated at not being able to learn more in the class.

The next semester Chozin was in a similar mixed undergraduate/graduate class with a large group project. This time, Chozin created a plan so that he could be successful in the course. He chose a topic early in the semester, and one that he had already learned something about in the previous term. Instead of becoming the last one to be chosen for a group, Chozin advertised his idea to his class. He was able to capitalize on undergraduate malaise to quickly form a group. This time *he* was the one with specialized knowledge of the topic and *he* was the one with a plan to help the group succeed. He had a more positive and more educational experience as a result.

His experience asks those of us who require group assignments to do some hard analysis of our classes. Are we setting international and multilingual students up for failure because they don't have the American cultural knowledge needed for a project? How are we ensuring that all members of a group are participating? Or that international and multilingual students are being treated with respect? Could we offer group assignments that would allow international and multilingual students to be the experts in the content and let them teach domestic students instead of creating situations where they have to be followers?

Dr. Talinn Phillips
Associate Professor of English
Ohio University

Chozin's experience and Talinn Phillips's reflections offer suggestions for how we can support students who might feel like outsiders in group projects or discussions. With planning and an eye for inclusivity, we can build assignments and activities that are more inviting for diverse students.

Supporting Student Interaction in the Global Classroom

Faculty have many tools at their disposal in terms of supporting connections between students. These include raising students' awareness of learning possibilities that they may be overlooking, raising awareness of how majority or mainstream attitudes can affect the participation of diverse student groups, and monitoring student interactions. Grouping students into "cohort-like" classrooms can help students connect (Kimmel & Volet, 2012), as can allowing students time to connect socially during class (Davies, 2009). In online discussions, smaller groups can yield more participation and more quality participation than large-class discussions (Bliss & Lawrence, 2009). Increasing social presence (or "the degree to which a person is perceived as a 'real person' in mediated communication"; Gunawardena, 1995, p. 151) in digital environments can help increase engagement and thus participation, as well as increase retention (Liu, Gomez, & Yen, 2009). In both online or face-to-face formats, group work or collaborations can range from analyzing case studies, to problem-based learning, project-based learning, or cooperative learning. In these contexts, working to maximize the potential that students from different backgrounds understand both each other *and* the content can be more complicated and therefore require teacher support and, if necessary, intervention.

The following *Case Study* highlights the importance of interactions and engagement, even when there is uncertainty about how projects will proceed or what skills will be required.

CASE STUDY: IT'S OK TO BE UNCOMFORTABLE

I teach on a regional campus, and most of our students work part- or full-time jobs and many have already started families in addition to their quest for a better education. Because of their many responsibilities, our students are less likely to study abroad or to interact with people from other countries. Living in a small community and not having opportunities or the financial ability to travel can impact one's worldview. In response, we began internationalizing the curriculum by introducing COIL (Collaborative Online International Learning). I was surprised that students seemed very uncomfortable about the idea of working with students from another country. I have always loved to travel and learn about new cultures.

The whole idea of class collaborations was very new to me. It sounded exciting but I was a little reticent myself. Would it work? What if it failed? With whom would I work? How would we navigate the cultural differences?

After getting university support and training as a newly named COIL Fellow, I was excited...and a bit scared! The first section of the training was wholly online. We had to answer many questionnaires in an effort to begin to find a partner—a match. It seemed a little like dating... and a bit nerve-wracking. But, I was elated the day I connected with someone and we decided to be partners. Our next job was to collaborate to fulfill modules for the training. We ran into time differences, vacation schedules, language differences, and miscommunications but we were successful in completing the course. The next step was flying to Cuernavaca, Mexico for additional training and to collaborate with my new-found partner. More nervousness ensued. SUNY made our travel plans and it was a little daunting flying alone to another country. To say I was nervous was an understatement.

In Cuernavaca, I found myself with twenty-nine other trainees in a retreat. I met my partner for the first time face-to-face and exchanged nervous laughter. Our trainer was fantastic and we spent the next four days getting to know one another and completing task after task to set up our syllabi and plan the minute details of our future class collaboration. I was absolutely fear-stricken to make a ten second video of myself welcoming my new students in Spanish but I survived and was proud when it was complete. I learned so much useful information for the classroom, two of the most important being:

1. Cross-cultural collaborations can be uncomfortable and uncertain sometimes.
2. Moving through the discomfort and uncertainty will give you renewed confidence in yourself.

My partner and I have had four classes collaborate over the last year. We understand when our students feel uncomfortable or uncertain because we felt that way ourselves. I can relate to students that it's perfectly okay to have these feelings. It's part of the process. Students have fears but they, too, work through them to find the rewards of learning more about and exploring other cultures. I found my fears about not being able to find anyone interested to work with me to be so unfounded in reality—there are so many teachers who understand the importance of globalizing the curriculum. This has been such a personally and professionally enriching experience. It's the things that make us uncomfortable that often change us the most.

Dr. Pamela Kaylor
Associate Lecturer of Communication Studies
and Women's, Gender, and Sexuality Studies
Ohio University-Lancaster

Pamela Kaylor's story reminds us that we are not alone. As we strive to help students engage and interact with each other meaningfully, we are reminded that sometimes we also can feel out of our depth. But that in itself can be useful as well. Her *Case Study* also highlights the potential of online platforms in providing students with opportunities to learn from and engage with individuals different from themselves.

After reflecting on our own experiences, expectations, and comfort levels with different participation-related questions, we can tackle participation from a variety of angles. Figure 5.1 illustrates several considerations, focusing on opportunities that faculty have in supporting participation between students who share different backgrounds or values. In addition to helping students build a connection in class, faculty can support students during their discussions or group work and can be clear and transparent in their expectations for learning and assessment.

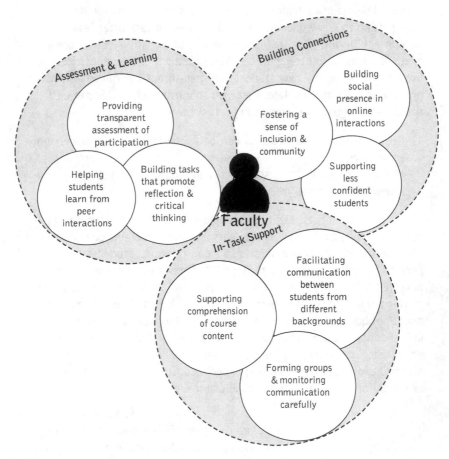

Figure 5.1 Facilitating Participation in the Global Classroom

CLASSROOM STRATEGIES

Classroom Strategies are structured around key questions. In this chapter, we offer a variety of strategies for increasing participation across diverse groups.

"How can I increase participation in my classes, particularly between students from different backgrounds or with students who need extra time with course content or expressing their ideas?"

Addressing participation begins with identifying possible reasons students aren't participating (see the *Key Concepts* section earlier in the chapter). Solutions are most effective when they are directly related to likely obstacle(s).

One often overlooked obstacle is in the definition of participation and its role in learning. Try starting your course by articulating your participation definition and expectations, why it is important, and how students will be assessed. Or, try asking students from different backgrounds and experiences how they define "participation." How do their definitions compare to each other and to yours?

Consider allowing definitions of participation besides answering questions in a large group (e.g., small-group work, technology such as discussion boards, journal entries). Try the following strategies to increase participation in your diverse class:

1. Increase Comprehension of Course Content
Students who understand content and expectations are more likely to participate. For example:

- *Monitor your speaking rate.* Try recording yourself or having a colleague observe a class and provide recommendations.
- *Monitor class comprehension.* While lecturing, monitor facial expressions and avoid slang, potentially unfamiliar words or metaphors, and culturally based humor or examples.
- *Ask detailed questions.* Comprehension questions that require students to demonstrate understanding (e.g., 1-minute papers explaining a concept) are more helpful than general questions (e.g., "Are there any questions?").
- *Use visuals students can return to.* Especially important are visuals for directions and vocabulary that may be unfamiliar. Offer multiple versions of the same information such as graphs, outlines, articles, or videos.

- *State activity objectives clearly.* Explain to students why you are doing the activity and how it relates to the class in general. Tie objectives to professional or career goals when possible.
- *Ensure students can hear and understand each other.* In larger classrooms or those with poor acoustics, or for quieter students, you can rephrase the question or comment, or ask the student to speak louder.
- *Use a one-sentence summary in large classes.* At the beginning, middle, or end of class, ask students to finish a sentence (e.g., of what happened to whom and when). Students can share their mini-summaries with a partner or turn them in as a formative assessment to guide future classes.

2. Build Support and Connection

Students who may not be as comfortable participating in large discussions benefit from strategies that allow for smaller and more supported tasks. For example:

- *Acknowledge diversity and be the expert.* Share with students strategies you use to build trust and open communication with people who share a different background or beliefs. Invite students to share their strategies and project a positive attitude about the diversity in your class.
- *Allow anonymous questions.* Try having students write questions on notecards that you collect as a group or use anonymous social media or polling software.
- *Wait after asking questions.* Let students write ideas or share answers prior to or instead of large group discussions.
- *Try think-pair-share.* Invite students to consider their own response before sharing with others; they then discuss ideas with a partner. Finally, students are called on or invited to share with the class.
- *Indicate genuine interest in students' comments.* Students are more likely to speak in class when they feel that the instructor and classmates appreciate their perspective. Build small to big—have smaller groups engage in a discussion task and invite volunteers to share with the larger group. Put comments on the screen or a whiteboard to showcase contributions. Start the course with questions that allow students to draw from their own backgrounds and experiences.
- *Use visuals or images to prompt discussion.* Students can choose from ones you provide or can bring their own to class. Visuals can allow you to guide students to notice similarities, not just differences.
- *Expand participation to include written as well as oral comments, for example through blogs, discussion boards, or social media.* It is not uncommon for some students to participate at higher rates in digital environments.

- *Break large classes into smaller groups for discussions and give students tasks or have them complete an online quiz after the activity.* Debates can be used for a more controlled discussion.
- *Try various seating options such as diversity seating* (peers sit next to classmates different from themselves), discipline seating (peers sit next to classmates from other majors), skills grouping (peers sit next to classmates with various areas of expertise), or assigned seating.
- *Call on students to answer.* Some students are very accustomed to waiting their turn and may expect to be called on.
- *Redirect students who make inconsiderate comments.* Ask students to provide examples or support for comments that reveal biases.
- *Let students teach each other.* Students can explain a concept they prepared in small groups, using posters, presentations, videos, or images. A gallery walk (where students explain posters or stations) allows students to practice their presentations several times with classmates who walk by.
- *Connect content to students' lives.* Ask students to connect classwork to their experiences or let them identify discussion topics. (See Brookfield, 1999, and Davis, 1993, for strategies for maintaining respectful discussions, ways to invite students to offer diverse views, and facilitating participation in large classes.)
- *Set expectations and monitor class dynamics.* Begin the course with a discussion on participation expectations, perhaps forming ground rules as a group. When students are allowed to pick their own partners, do they voluntarily mix themselves up or stay in their own groups? Do students seem to be asking each other questions about class instead of asking you?
- *Ask questions that require more complex answers, for example ones that require analysis, compare/contrast, cause/effect, or clarification.* Try to avoid rhetorical, yes/no, leading, or vague questions.

3. Grade Participation Carefully

Consider how you are using participation grades and how effective for learning they may be for your less vocal students. Consider trying the following:

- *Do not grade participation.* Instead, focus on encouraging students to participate without needing the grade. Demonstrate to your students how participating and engaging in course activities benefits their learning and classmates' learning as well. Try grading participation indirectly by creating graded assignments or in-class tasks that require collaboration. (See Czekanski & Wolf, 2013, for research on grading participation.)

113

- *Provide clear guidelines in the syllabus on how the grade is calculated.* Try giving students a participation rubric or scale, or using polling software (e.g., Kahoot, PollEverywhere, Mentimeter) that records student names to start off in-class discussions. In addition to evaluating quantity, characteristics such as dependability and quality (which includes respectful comments) can also be considered. If using a rubric, a space to deduct points for interrupting a classmate can be included in order to build inclusion (Yaylacı & Beauvais, 2017).
- *Have students evaluate their own or their peers' participation.* Students can reflect on how their out-of-class preparation affects their in-class participation, such as asking them to rate themselves as being fully engaged, occasionally engaged, disengaged, or needing direction. If students rate peer participation, extra faculty planning and a strong classroom rapport are often required. Peer or self-evaluation of participation may be more effective as a reflection tool for students than for a grade.

4. Build Social Presence and a Culture of Respect Online

Students with higher feelings of social presence in online classes are more likely to stay in the course and score passing grades (Liu et al., 2009). Faculty can encourage a sense of presence online through the following:

- *Build in personalized self-introductions.* Have students post brief bios with photos or videos of themselves and their own lives or backgrounds (e.g., with their families or pets, doing hobbies).
- *Build in active learning experiences (see Marmon, 2018).*
- *Utilize interactive online learning tools.* Interactive tools (e.g., Google Docs, VoiceThread, Padlet) allow students to communicate more naturally and create, share, or comment on various media (e.g., images, documents, audio or video files) via text or audio recordings.
- *Interact in real time.* If working in similar time zones, utilize synchronous (real-time) communication tools for students to interact or for virtual office hours, such as through chat or video conferencing with screen share options (e.g., with Zoom or Skype). Synchronous communication can complement activities with asynchronous (not time-bound) tools (e.g., discussion boards).
- *Communicate often.* Frequent communication from the instructor allows students to stay engaged and aware of expectations.
- *Personalize feedback when possible.* Audio or video feedback can require less time from the instructor and can raise social presence.

- *Monitor students' online communication.* Scan discussions for positive key words that reveal learning and reflection, or concerning words relating to frustration, isolation, or falling behind.
- *Focus on ideas students express.* Grade participation in online discussions on quality over number of responses. A participation portfolio approach can be used to encourage students to reflect on their course-long contributions (Nilson & Goodson, 2017).

Increasing participation in diverse classes requires careful planning. The following *Case Study* by an African American professor highlights the importance of faculty persistence in helping students build the trust they will need in order to listen to peers different from themselves.

CASE STUDY: HELPING STUDENTS TRUST EACH OTHER

I gained one of the most valued instructional lessons of my academic career in an upper-level American politics course. It focused on the influences of social identities upon historical and contemporary life experiences. My experiences teaching this class shaped, informed, and challenged me as a professor to intentionally be more flexible with my pedagogical strategies—I wanted to create an adaptive learning context that allows students the "space" to openly challenge the perspectives of their peers in order to develop an awareness and consciousness of different cultures and social groups. I had taught this class before at a private, elite women's university with students from diverse racial and ethnic backgrounds and they were very engaged and interested. But now I was teaching it at a co-ed public university which had a high degree of traditional homogeneity, although clearly it was in a transitional period reflective of growing diversity. This presented a different type of challenge for me.

In the co-ed public university, I found deep-seated perspectives about intergroup relations and realities in the United States. Students seemed unwilling to recognize the value and experiences of diverse viewpoints, at times engaging in extremely blatant emotional interactions laced with outright frustrations. Students differed widely in their perceptions about social, economic, and political conditions. While many believed in the supremacy of dominant viewpoints, ethnocentric attitudes, and gendered norms, others representing the

115

minority view forcefully challenged these dominant views and felt alienated and unappreciated.

Such emotionally charged discussions prompted me to take a proactive stance to ensure a positive learning experience for all students. First, I scheduled individual conferences to inquire about their learning experiences and to emphasize the necessity of respecting diverse opinions. During class, I challenged students to consider the positions of their peers and to actively think about their own worldviews relative to their colleagues. Second, to encourage more positive intercultural communication, I paired each student with another student who was clearly different in terms of identity and ideology. I asked them to have a 10-minute conversation on a potentially controversial topic and to write down points of agreement and disagreement acquired through the discussion. Finally, I carried out a post assessment and culminating class discussion, which revealed that while they were not necessarily fully accounting for the other perspective, eventually the majority of students acknowledged the value of diverse viewpoints and appreciated their growth in intergroup relations, intercultural understanding, and political thought.

By the end of the course, students recognized the legitimacy of opposing views and advocated for alternative perspectives during discussion. By the end, together, we had created a productive and effective learning environment.

Dr. Linda Trautman
Associate Professor of Political Science
Ohio University-Lancaster

Linda Trautman's story shows not only students' journeys as they learn to develop a global perspective and become more willing to engage with people and viewpoints different from themselves, but also a faculty journey as she experimented with innovative strategies to meet her course and personal goals.

"How can I help students from different backgrounds communicate and learn from each other in their group projects or collaborations?"

Given that less successful collaborations can lead to serious classroom concerns, it's important for faculty to plan carefully. Additionally, increased experiences with facilitating groups can lead to greater confidence and experimentation. The following suggestions address concerns that arise from group work projects (e.g., increased planning time, imbalances in student participation, communication problems, individual dislike for group work, unclear grading procedures). There are a variety of strategies that can facilitate integration and group work:

1. Consider Group Formation

- *Student surveys, observations, assignments, and grades can inform the formation of groups.* Considering student background, learning styles, and personality styles, in addition to content knowledge or experiences, is often beneficial. Or, if the goal is to form groups quickly, free online tools such as a random number or team name generators can be used.
- *Decide on timing.* Be clear if the group will work together for the entire term or if groups will change.
- *Experiment with group size and composition.* Three or four students per group increases participation opportunities. The whole class can work in smaller groups on the same problem and then debrief together; each group can be given a different problem and then debrief together; or each group can be given a different problem, new groups can be formed for another round of discussion, and conclude with a debriefing.

2. Assign Clear Group Tasks with a Reflective Component

- *Establish clear guidelines and put those expectations in writing (e.g., regarding assignments, time limits, group participation, feedback, and grades).* Clear directions and tasks lead to more concrete learning outcomes and smoother group communication.
- *Assign projects that require collaboration for success.* Ideally, students realize that working together leads to more learning and/or a better product.
- *Use group tasks to build connection.* Group tasks can be used to highlight similarities within the group, or students can be asked to do a self-analysis of their own personality types before engaging in more time-intensive and graded group projects. These self-assessments can lead to greater awareness of individual contributions and also areas of potential conflict and possible communication strategies.

3. Facilitate and Monitor Group Communication

- *Ask students to write group ground rules.* These can be regarding assignments and work or behavior expectations. In the ground rules, ask students to include consequences if desired behaviors don't occur.

- *Monitor group communication during class.* Circulate the room, join groups, or give short in-class surveys or open-ended questions.
- *Train students to monitor their group communication.* Students can be guided to monitor their own group dynamics, such as the level of trust within the group (see Kaar, 2010, pp. 100–103).
- *Guide students to move beyond their comfort zone.* Students can take on various roles in groups (e.g., leader, reporter, timekeeper, spokesperson) and those roles can either be constant or rotate. Requiring students to rotate through the roles allows for opportunities for growth as they move out of their comfort zones. Asking thought-provoking questions that invite discussion and reflection (e.g., "What is your goal for…?"; "How does this relate to…?"; "How do we measure…?") and allowing group members to answer each other is often key to successful communication.
- *Teach students group communication strategies.* If a class is struggling with teamwork, groups can discuss challenges and possible solutions in a whole-class meeting. Teams can also be taught strategies that encourage listening and critical thinking, such as the FSLC technique:

  F = formulate an answer on your own
  S = share your answer on your own
  L = listen carefully to your partner's answer
  C = create a new answer that is superior to your individual answers.

4. Assess Group Communication and Student Perceptions

- *Consider assessing the group communication as well as the actual group product.* Group communication can be assessed via peer assessments, which can occur midterm or term-final and include write-ups or surveys, evaluation forms, or in-person conversations with questions focusing on timeliness, work quality, attitude, and personal goals. (See Ohland et al., 2012 for a sample questionnaire.)
- *Require individual reflection assignments.* Ongoing assignments such as journals allow for input on individual participation.
- *Use a grading rubric that is customized to the assignment and give the rubric to teams early in the process.* All members can receive the same grade, individuals can receive a grade for their portion only, or a combination of these strategies can be used.
- *Gather student perceptions of class and group work, such as collecting midterm feedback.* Students can be asked to list on a notecard what they *Like, Don't*

Like, and *Want More Of*. Or, students can complete a midterm course evaluation online. Either way, a class discussion and possible course changes can follow.

 THE WORKSHOP

5.1 Inviting a Colleague to Observe Student Participation

Inviting a colleague to observe can be very useful given the realities of the classroom or lab environment; for example, you cannot observe all students while also teaching, or monitor all group discussions simultaneously. Your colleague can take note of how many students participate and any nonverbal cues that might indicate an area of concern. They can also observe for the presence or absence of behaviors indicating a global perspective.

See the Student Participation Checklist below and modify it as needed. Discussion with your peer before and after the observation can lead to increased feedback. Including students in discussions on this topic can lead to new and customized strategies as well.

Total number of students (either in class or group):_____

Number of students who contributed more than just slightly:_____

Student Participation Checklist	Students...		
	need considerable work/not apparent	have room to grow in this area	are strong in this area
Open-mindedness Comments and behaviors demonstrate ability to assess own worldview and willingness to consider classmates' opinions based on the evidence they provide; willingness to consider views that are inconsistent with their own opinions and to think from others' perspectives; and respectfully express a healthy skepticism of others' views that depict groups too narrowly or encourage "us vs. them" mindsets.			

Student Participation Checklist	Students...		
	need considerable work/not apparent	have room to grow in this area	are strong in this area
Anticipation of Complexity Comments look beyond simplistic explanations and acknowledge more complicated, interrelated factors.			
Comment Quality Comment contributes to the discussion by moving the discussion forward, providing a new perspective or example, raising a valid concern, or synthesizing points. Students appear to be prepared for discussion and are not raising unrelated or overly general points. Comments build on previous points; questions are relevant and invite critical thinking and discussion.			
Student Comfort Students appear comfortable in participating. Students volunteer.			
Student Listening Non-speaking students appear to be listening (e.g., following speakers, nodding or other nonverbal behavior) and do not appear to be offended by any comments or feel shut out.			
Range of Students More than just a handful of students participate.			
Other			

Next, jot down potential reasons that students may not be participating (in online or face-to-face classes) and also strategies to implement in order to address the concerns.

Possible reasons students don't participate in class	Strategies to increase participation, and notes on effectiveness

5.2 Planning for Successful Participation

Consider a class that has concerned you regarding student participation, group work, or integration between various groups. What comments would you like students to write on their course evaluations about how they feel about the course in terms of connection to peers or to you, or in terms of learning from each other? What specific strategies can you try in order to increase the likelihood that you actually receive those types of comments?

Complete the following table on comments you would like to see in future student course evaluations, as well as obstacles you may encounter and strategies to try.

Topic Area	Comments I Want from Students	Obstacles or Problem Areas	In-class Strategies to Try
Classroom Environment			
Learning from Peers			
Experiences with Group Work			

Topic Area	Comments I Want from Students	Obstacles or Problem Areas	In-class Strategies to Try
Integration across Groups			
Comprehensibility of Lectures or Directions			

DISCUSSION AND REFLECTION

1. What factors do you think have the greatest influence on your students' participation?
2. Refer back to Figure 5.1 (Facilitating Participation in Global Classrooms). In which areas might your students benefit from more support or more intentionality on your part as the course facilitator?
3. Reflect on the *Case Studies* in this chapter. What types of participation activities or support can you plan for your students based on the experiences of others?
4. It's not uncommon for faculty to feel that students' increased dependence on smart phones and social media leads to decreased motivation in the classroom, increased distraction, and thus lowered participation. What role do you feel technology plays in your courses in overall student participation? How can you structure your class time in order to maximize student interest and increase participation in spite of the presence of their devices?
5. Sometimes faculty or departments that build inclusivity and a global perspective in their courses experience increases in enrollment by more diverse students. What challenges and opportunities might you experience in class if you had a greater number of non-mainstream students, and are you prepared for this?

BIBLIOGRAPHY

Andrade, M. (2006). International students in English-speaking universities: Adjustment factors. *Journal of Research in International Education, 5*, 131–154.

Bliss, C., & Lawrence, B. (2009). Is the whole greater than the sum of its parts? A comparison of small group and whole class discussion board activity in online courses. *Journal of Asynchronous Learning Networks, 13*(4), 25–39.

Brookfield, S. (1999). *Discussion as a way of teaching*. San Francisco, CA: Jossey-Bass.

Czekanski, K., & Wolf, Z. (2013). Encouraging and evaluating class participation. *Journal of University Teaching & Learning Practice, 10*(1).

Davies, W. (2009). Group work as a form of assessment: Common problems and recommended solutions. *The International Journal of Higher Education and Educational Planning*, *58*, 563–584.

Davis, B. (1993). *Tools for teaching*. San Francisco, CA: Jossey-Bass.

Fozdar, F., & Volet, S. (2012). Intercultural learning among community development students: Positive attitudes, ambivalent experiences. *Community Development*, *43*(3), 361–378.

Fritschner, L. (2000). Inside the undergraduate college classroom: Faculty and students differ on the meaning of student participation. *The Journal of Higher Education*, 71(3), 342–362.

Gerzon, M. (2010). *Global citizens: How our vision of the world is outdated, and what we can do about it*. London, UK: Rider.

Glass, C. (2012). Educational experiences associated with international students' learning, development, and positive perceptions of campus climate. *Journal of Studies in International Education*, *16*(3), 228–251.

Gunawardena, C. (1995). Social presence theory and implications for interaction and collaborative learning in computer conferences. *International Journal of Educational Telecommunications*, *1*(2/3), 147–166.

Hall, R., & Sandler, B. (1982). *The classroom climate: A chilly one for women?* Project on the Status and Education of Women, February. Washington, DC: Association of American Colleges.

Kaar, A. (2010). Emotional management: Expressing, interpreting, and making meaning of feelings in multicultural teams. In M. Guilherme, E. Glaser, & M. Méndez-García (Eds.), *The intercultural dynamics of multicultural working* (pp. 95–108). Bristol, UK: Multilingual Matters.

Killick, D. (2015). *Developing the global student: Higher education in an era of globalization*. London, UK: Routledge.

Kimmel, K., & Volet, S. (2012). University students' perceptions of and attitudes towards culturally diverse group work: Does context matter? *Journal of Studies in International Education*, *16*(2), 157–181.

Kuh, G. (2009). The National Survey of Student Engagement: Conceptual and empirical foundations. *New Directions for Institutional Research*, 141, 5–20.

Lave, J., & Wenger, E. (1998). *Situated learning: Legitimate peripheral participation*. Cambridge, UK: Cambridge University Press.

Liu, S., Gomez, J., & Yen, C. (2009). Community college online course retention and final grade: Predictability of social presence. *Journal of Interactive Online Learning*, *8*(2), 165–182.

Marmon, M. (2018). *Enhancing social presence in online learning environments*. Hershey, PA: IGI Global.

Meyer, K. (2009). Student classroom engagement: Rethinking participation grades and student silence (Unpublished doctoral dissertation). Ohio University, Athens, OH.

Moore, P., & Hampton, G. (2015). 'It's a bit of a generalisation, but...': Participant perspectives on intercultural group assessment in higher education. *Assessment & Evaluation in Higher Education*, *40*(3), 390–406.

Nilson, L., & Goodson, L. (2017). *Online teaching at its best: Merging instructional design with teaching and learning research*. San Francisco, CA: Jossey-Bass.

Ohland, M., Loughry, M., Woehr, D., Bullard, L., Felder, R., Finelli, ... & Schmucker, D. (2012). Comprehensive assessment of team member effectiveness: Development of a behaviorally anchored rating scale for self- and peer evaluation. *Academy of Management Learning & Education*, *11*(4), 609–630.

Phillips, T. (2008). Examining bridges, expanding boundaries, imagining new identities: The writing center as bridge for second language graduate writers (Unpublished doctoral dissertation). Ohio University, Athens, OH.

Stoynoff, S. (1997). Factors associated with international students' academic achievement. *Journal of Instructional Psychology*, *24*(1), 56–68.

Takahashi, S., & Saito, E. (2013). Unraveling the process and meaning of problem-based learning experiences. *Higher Education*, *66*, 693–706.

Tatar, S. (2005). Classroom participation by international students: The case of Turkish graduate students. *Journal of Studies in International Education*, *9*(4), 337–355.

Yaylacı, S., & Beauvais, E. (2017). The role of social group membership on classroom participation. *PS: Political Science & Politics*, *50*(2), 559–564.

Chapter 6

Designing Writing Assignments for Global Citizens

 INTRODUCTION

In this chapter, we introduce some key principles of writing pedagogy and effective assignment design while also highlighting relationships between writing and a global perspective. Writing projects encourage students to engage in deep, sustained thinking about a particular idea or problem and can also easily be designed to encourage self-reflection. Writing projects are therefore a valuable way to assess students' global perspective; yet in order for writing projects to be effective, as faculty we need to adopt a global perspective ourselves, making both our assignments and our response to writing accessible to a variety of students. This chapter will help ensure you are using a global perspective when you create writing assignments and offer ideas for using writing to support learning.

While we advocate incorporating writing into the curriculum in substantial ways, we also recognize that curricular constraints, the strengths of individual instructors, and faculty workloads are real barriers. Thus, we've included a range of strategies that can be implemented based on context. One of this chapter's goals is to move faculty to a critical assessment of the writing in their curricula and then *strategically* integrate more writing as appropriate. By the end of this chapter, faculty should have ideas for integrating writing into courses in ways that provide all students, regardless of language background, with an opportunity to demonstrate their strengths.

By the end of this chapter, you should be able to:

- assess the writing within your existing curriculum;
- make distinctions between formal and informal writing and describe the value of each;
- identify existing writing assignments that could prove problematic for multilingual and other diverse learners;

- develop writing assignments that are accessible for all students; and
- identify existing writing assignments that inadvertently facilitate plagiarism and make them plagiarism-resistant.

 ## CLASSROOM AND SELF-ASSESSMENT

Before working through the *Key Concepts* on writing, spend a few moments reflecting on the role that writing plays within your classes and within your larger program or department. If necessary, talk to other faculty in your program or conduct a quick scan of syllabi to make your assessment.

 ## ASSESSING THE ROLE OF WRITING IN YOUR OWN CLASSES

In this chapter, we examine the role that effective writing assignments can play in a globalized classroom. First, it's useful to understand where writing currently exists in your curriculum, both personally and programmatically.

In my large classes, I typically ask students to:

★	do no writing at all.
★ ★	compose some short answer/essay questions on tests and other assignments.
★ ★ ★	engage in some less formal writing to process their learning experiences, for example journals, "minute papers," response papers OR compose a formal writing project.
★ ★ ★ ★	engage in some less formal writing to process their learning experiences, for example journals, "minute papers," response papers AND compose one or more formal writing projects.

In my regular classes (20–45 students), I typically ask students to:

★	do no writing at all.
★ ★	compose some short answer/essay questions on tests and other assignments.

★ ★ ★	engage in some less formal writing to process their learning experiences, for example journals, "minute papers," response papers OR compose a formal writing project.
★ ★ ★ ★	engage in some less formal writing to process their learning experiences, for example journals, "minute papers," response papers AND compose one or more formal writing projects.

In my small classes, I typically ask students to:

★	do no writing at all.
★ ★	compose some short answer/essay questions on tests, etc.
★ ★ ★	engage in some less formal writing to process their learning experiences, for example journals, "minute papers," response papers OR compose a formal writing project.
★ ★ ★ ★	engage in some less formal writing to process their learning experiences, for example journals, "minute papers," response papers AND compose one or more formal writing projects.

ASSESSING THE ROLE OF WRITING IN YOUR PROGRAM OR DEPARTMENT

In our large and general education classes, our program typically asks students to:

★	do no writing at all.
★ ★	compose some short answer/essay questions on tests, etc.
★ ★ ★	engage in some less formal writing to process their learning experiences, for example journals, "minute papers," response papers, OR compose a formal writing project.
★ ★ ★ ★	engage in some less formal writing to process their learning experiences, for example journals, "minute papers," response papers, AND compose one or more formal writing projects.

In our classes for majors, our program typically asks students to:

★	do no writing at all.
★ ★	compose some short answer/essay questions on tests, etc.
★ ★ ★	engage in some less formal writing to process their learning experiences, for example journals, "minute papers," response papers, OR compose a formal writing project.
★ ★ ★ ★	engage in some less formal writing to process their learning experiences, for example journals, "minute papers," response papers, AND compose one or more formal writing projects.

In our seminars and capstone courses, our program typically asks students to:

★	do no writing at all.
★ ★	compose some short answer/essay questions on tests, etc.
★ ★ ★	engage in some less formal writing to process their learning experiences, for example journals, "minute papers," response papers, OR compose a formal writing project.
★ ★ ★ ★	engage in some less formal writing to process their learning experiences, for example journals, "minute papers," response papers, AND compose one or more formal writing projects.

 ## KEY CONCEPTS

As you may have gathered from the assessments, this chapter is grounded in two research-based principles. The first is the recognition that students will not master writing by taking the one or two classes that are part of most US undergraduate curricula. Writing is a long-term developmental process that is also highly contextual (Adler-Kassner & Wardle, 2016). One course simply isn't enough time, nor can it possibly prepare students for the range of genres and disciplinary conventions they'll encounter. Moreover, international students will often have had far less exposure to academic writing or writing instruction than their domestic peers. Second, there are many ways for a curriculum to support students' writing development, from formal writing projects that receive thoughtful, intensive instructor response to very informal projects that may not be graded at all. Everything on this spectrum can support students' writing development.

Writing as a Developmental Process

Learning to write academic English successfully is a long-term project for all of us, regardless of cultural or educational backgrounds. Even proficient writers often face setbacks when introduced to unfamiliar genres (e.g., a first grant proposal). These challenges are even greater for multilingual and other diverse students. Students who did not attend US high schools may never have taken a writing course or received any kind of writing instruction. Or, all of the writing instruction they have received may have been focused on short exercises to pass standardized tests. The research is also quite clear that it takes those who are still learning English much longer to compose than it takes native English-speaking students (Silva, 1993).

Even among domestic students who are native speakers of English, academic writing is still very challenging. While no one speaks "Standard" Academic English natively, our home dialects may be closer or further away from the "standard." Students who speak varieties that are often stigmatized, such as Black or Appalachian English, may be at a particular disadvantage. Domestic students, regardless of race or class, will have had varying preparation during high school and few enter university prepared to engage in the analytical writing typically required.

Writing is a developmental process that simply takes time to master. We often like to hope that the English Department has already fully prepared students. Unfortunately, this is not possible; students need time and exposure to a variety of writing tasks, including opportunities to revise based on feedback. Students also need to learn to write for their future fields, a process that disciplinary faculty are best prepared to support. Thus, there are a variety of issues to attend to when designing writing assignments in today's global classroom: language ability, general writing experience, knowledge of the discipline, and genre-specific writing experience.

The Formal–Informal Writing Continuum

This chapter's second foundational concept is that writing projects can be classified on a continuum of formal to informal writing. Faculty are no doubt familiar with formal projects; these are traditional "term papers," although other kinds of writing projects are formal as well. Students may also be asked to build a website, publish a magazine, or submit a letter to the editor. Well-designed, formal projects are high-stakes and involve drafting, receiving feedback, and revising. Correctness is also important in formal projects, especially when there is an audience beyond the classroom. Finally, formal projects are often designed for students to *demonstrate* their knowledge as they apply course concepts or report the findings of research.

In contrast, the primary purpose of informal writing projects is for students to *generate* knowledge. Students may be asked to journal about their experiences in a service-learning class, they may write response papers to articles, or they may write a "minute paper" or summary after a lecture. Since informal projects are designed to help students generate knowledge by learning more deeply, correctness often isn't an important criterion. Informal work may not be collected or graded or it may only be shared with peers. We are not suggesting that teachers should never grade or respond to informal work, only recognizing that students can benefit from the process of writing even without receiving a response.

When teachers do respond to informal work, that response may be minimal and only focus on meeting basic criteria for the assignment. Or, response to informal work may start a conversation with the writer without assessing it. Formal projects, on the other hand, usually involve a substantial investment of student time and thus call for a careful evaluation from the instructor. Both kinds of response are important, but both are not necessary for every assignment.

Writing assignments are valuable for student learning, whether asking students to generate or demonstrate knowledge. However, the reality of faculty workloads in large classes or among those with heavy workloads means that faculty may need students to demonstrate knowledge in ways that are less time-consuming to grade. In such cases, it is still often worthwhile to require informal writing to help students deepen their content knowledge; teachers may then provide minimal feedback or use that writing during the class to foster discussion, etc. without grading it.

Challenges of Composing in an Additional Language

There are a number of important differences between writing in a first language and writing in a second/additional language. When people write in a second language, it takes them much more time to generate text and their writing is typically judged to be less successful than the writing of native speakers (Silva, 1993). Language learners also make more errors and most will have a "written accent" no matter how much time and energy they've spent studying the language (Silva, 1993).

Those of us who teach multilingual writers also need to be aware that international students may have had little or no writing instruction in their previous academic careers (Russell & Foster, 2002). They may have been taught how to write a short essay for a test, but that doesn't mean they're familiar with the specialized genres of academia or that they've written substantial texts before. Multilingual students also may not yet have the vocabulary required to read academic texts or listen to academic lectures effectively.

While multilingual students certainly face challenges when writing in a second language, they also have important resources that domestic students often lack. They bring resources from entirely different language(s) and culture(s). They've learned, even if informally, other rhetorical strategies that they may be able to employ successfully in English. They also have the resilience and persistence necessary to become competent in a new language and to study outside of their home cultures. These are traits that many monolingual domestic students may have never had the opportunity to develop. In the *Student Voice* below, Lana Oweidat shares how she wrestled with the traditional US rhetorical convention of "put the thesis first" and how she ultimately used her Arabic rhetorical knowledge as a valuable part of her pre-writing and drafting work in US academic texts.

STUDENT VOICE: NAVIGATING LINGUISTIC AND CULTURAL HURDLES AS A SECOND LANGUAGE ACADEMIC WRITER

As a second language writer, my journey in writing academically in English was riddled with successes and challenges while I learned to navigate between languages, genres, and ideas. Toward the beginning of this journey, I began all my writing in English with an exploratory mode in tandem with how I write in my native language, Arabic. This exploratory mode resisted an introductory thesis, instead waiting until the end and allowing ample time for the exploration of the topic. In other words, I used a specific genre of English writing, but one that was close to how I wrote in my native language. From a linguistic perspective, I was more at ease knowing I could write "AraboEnglish" in a genre that allowed for code-meshing [mixing languages], because it was, by definition, about authorial exploration rather than rigidity. As a reader-responsible language, Arabic allows for poetic prose and ambiguity, which worked well with the exploratory mode that I chose to write in. Next came the phase where I re-envisioned the text, revised it and moved my thesis to the beginning, as well as rephrased sentences and support to give them an evidentiary, rather than emotional, basis. Although my level of ease in writing academically in English increased with time and practice, the real challenge occurred when I navigated the rhetorical situation of my dissertation.

Many think of their dissertation committees as the audience for their dissertations. While this was true in my case, I couldn't help but think of another audience: my possible future Jordanian employer. Since I thought I'd apply for jobs in both the US and Jordan, this influenced what I included in my dissertation and how I discussed certain topics. For example, certain political issues and some discussions of religion, sex, and gender have to be dealt with carefully for a Jordanian audience. While writing to these multiple audiences and being true to my beliefs and the scholarship in the fields I drew from in my dissertation, I developed certain strategies to navigate that tension. For example, I became better at circling around some issues and learned to be more comfortable with ambiguity while still delivering good work that pleased my Western audience. This maneuvering very much describes my journey as a beginning and advanced academic writer of the English language: consistently thinking about how forms and topics function differently in various discourses, in order to find a middle ground that works for the in-betweenness of my positionality.

Dr. Lana Oweidat
Assistant Professor of Rhetoric and Composition
Goucher College

Understanding the Complexities of Plagiarism

After working to design effective assignments, there are few things more disheartening to faculty than identifying plagiarism. Although there is no way to eliminate plagiarism, there are strategies that make it more difficult for students to plagiarize and to encourage them to do the work instead of taking shortcuts.

First, though, we need to clarify exactly what plagiarism means. The term is usually defined as something like *word thief*. The use of *thief* contributes to the moral and even criminal connotations injected into US discussions of plagiarism. In some cases, students do buy papers from others, share papers, or make a paper out of blatant copy-and-paste work from the Internet. This is clearly cheating and should be treated accordingly.

Most of the time though, the moralizing surrounding poor textual borrowing isn't very helpful, largely because "stealing others' words" is a very Western cultural concept. The idea that words or ideas can be *owned* by someone and then *stolen* is completely foreign in most cultures—even absurd. International students have probably been introduced to plagiarism during orientation, but they may not have a very deep understanding of what plagiarism is, how to avoid it, or why their professors care about it so much. Even when international students have a reasonable understanding of plagiarism and successfully avoid it, it doesn't mean that they value the principles behind it or see it as a great failure. Even domestic students who are well versed in the consequences of plagiarism may not have truly learned how to avoid it. They have often internalized meaningless "rules" like "As long as I change every third word then I'm paraphrasing" instead of actually learning to recreate others' ideas accurately.

The primary problem with punishing poor paraphrasing is that the criterion of "too close to the original" is a very elastic, subjective one. There are no rules about how many words are allowed to "match," how close the sentence structure can remain, etc. This is not to say that there aren't clear cases of poor paraphrasing and that students need to improve, but only that there is no clearly defined standard for them to work toward. Paraphrasing is a complex task, requiring the paraphraser to have a sophisticated knowledge of the source text, which can be especially challenging with academic texts or when a writer is new to a discipline. Writers may not have the reading ability and strength of vocabulary to craft an appropriate paraphrase; simply telling the writer that the paraphrase is "too close" won't be enough to change that. When writers paraphrase poorly, faculty might first look at writers' citation practices. If they are citing appropriately, that is evidence that they were trying to do the right thing and have at least met the reader's needs by providing citations.

Second, the moralizing surrounding the term *plagiarism* also attempts to criminalize and shame normal learning. Above, we used the term *textual borrowing* because that is what plagiarism actually is: borrowing from others' texts. All academic writers borrow from others' texts; the question is whether that borrowing is successful, helping to strengthen the writer's argument and reputation, or whether it is unsuccessful. Moreover, successful borrowing is context-dependent; the US academy has a list of conventions for acknowledging another's influence on a text but employing MLA citation would be ridiculous in a political speech. We have different conventions for acknowledging sources in those contexts. Students will need to learn the conventions of textual borrowing in the academy and, as in most things, they will likely learn by doing it badly at first.

To help explain how ineffective textual borrowing reveals students' learning, Howard (1999) introduced the concept of *patchwriting*, or "copying from a source text and then deleting some words, altering grammatical structures, or plugging in one synonym for another" (xvii). Howard presents a history of patchwriting— a history which grows out of ancient practices of imitation, not deception—and offers a much more nuanced explanation of patchwriting.

It is a process of evaluating a source text, selecting passages pertinent to the patchwriter's purposes, and transporting those passages to the patchwriter's new context. Patchwriting accomplishes a (re)formation of a source text by providing a new locale and thus new meaning for source material [...].

133

> Patchwriting belongs not in a category with cheating on exams and purchasing term papers, but in a category with the ancient tradition of learning through apprenticeship and mimicry.
>
> (Howard, 1999, p. xviii)

Howard highlights the complicated succession of choices a student makes when patchwriting and, consequently, the understanding and learning that must take place in order for a student to write so "unsuccessfully." She argues that "absent any evidence of unethical authorial intention, the default category for patchwriting should be learning" and calls for faculty to take a more nuanced approach to charges of plagiarism—not in order to let students off the hook, but to support their learning (p. xxii).

 ## CLASSROOM STRATEGIES

"How should I design writing assignments?"

Strong assignments typically ask students to engage in an authentic task. This might mean conceiving projects similar to those actually conducted in the discipline (or developmentally appropriate versions that become more complex over time). For example, if writing proposals is a standard practice, then students should also learn how to write proposals during your program. An authentic task also asks students to engage in complex intellectual work and higher-order thinking (e.g., solving problems, proposing solutions, synthesizing multiple points of view). An authentic task "takes [students] beyond their current level of expertise, and diversifies their rhetorical and stylistic repertoires" (Ferris & Hedgcock, 2014, p. 127).

In contrast, inauthentic tasks are ones like five-paragraph essays and book reports. These kinds of tasks ask students to produce made-for-school genres that don't have much wider applicability or ask students to engage in much higher-order thinking.

Once you've identified a good task, Crusan (2010, p. 68) offers a simple heuristic for developing writing prompts.

1. Provide a brief context for the assignment (e.g., one or two sentences).
2. Specify the genre, audience, and general topic.
3. Use representative verbs to help students understand the target genre and rhetorical arrangement (e.g., argue, compare, contrast, synthesize, evaluate, etc.).

Since Crusan's heuristic is focused on in-class writing assignments, we would add that faculty should also specify procedural details like length, due dates, and citation system as well as any resources to be used (or avoided) and a rationale for the assignment. For a more detailed list, see Ferris and Hedgcock (2014, p. 127).

Most important, find a colleague to give you feedback on your drafted assignment. Inevitably, others are able to find holes, contradictions, and ambiguities in our assignments. Like us, no doubt you'll also continue to improve your assignments over time. When you realize you've inadvertently created a significant problem in your assignment, don't be afraid to revise it immediately *as long as* doing so doesn't disadvantage students.

"What informal assignments could deepen my students' learning?"

Below are several writing-to-learn activities that can easily be incorporated into many disciplines and courses. For further ideas and examples of grading rubrics, see Bean's (2011) *Engaging Ideas* or contact your campus's Writing across the Curriculum program, writing center, or English Department.

- *Blogging*, *online discussion boards*, and *inkshedding* are simple tools that can be either in-class or out-of-class work. Inkshedding is essentially an analog blog. One student responds to a prompt on paper and then passes the inkshed on to a new student who reads and comments further. The inkshed thus becomes a written discussion similar to a discussion board or blog. When completed before class, any of these tools can serve as reading checks and prepare students for discussion. After class, they can help students synthesize the day's learning. Prompts might ask students to reflect on a reading or a course concept or pose class discussion questions.
- *Response papers* have comparable uses, but without an interactive element. Response papers often ask students to summarize a reading or analyze it in some way, including the writer's personal reaction to the reading's ideas. Response papers are usually more formal than the activities above, simply because they are completed by one student outside of class. As a result, students are likely to expect feedback and engagement with their ideas and more formalized grading criteria.
- *Minute papers* are assigned to students at the end of class and are collected immediately. They might ask students to quickly summarize key points from class or to identify concepts that students still haven't grasped. Minute papers ask students to put their new learning to immediate use and serve as valuable comprehension checks.
- *Social media* provides engaging writing spaces while also helping students master particular genres and technologies that are valued by employers.

135

Faculty might use social media to encourage discussion beyond class, to allow students to contribute to the course by posting relevant news stories, or to check students' comprehension of course material. Video-based social media platforms ask students to develop new kinds of digital composing skills, drawing on students' existing competencies as print composers. These platforms may also be less stressful for students who can speak more easily than they can write; however, other students may find it challenging to compose in audio and video.

Each of these activities has multiple uses but is especially well suited to assessing a student's global perspective. For instance, asking a globally oriented discussion question in class elicits responses from two or three students, but having the class respond to that same question through a blog, discussion board, or social media provides responses from the entire class. *Journals* are a final option that encourage students to engage in personal reflection while also tracking the development of their thinking over time. Journals could be an excellent learning tool in a class that has a substantial global component.

"How can I design inclusive writing assignments for multilingual students?"

Many multilingual students will have had less exposure to dominant US culture than their domestic peers. As a result, they may struggle with assignments that require them to draw on cultural knowledge because they simply haven't acquired that knowledge. Moreover, some students may have no desire to acquire it. Students are studying in US institutions, but that may not be entirely by choice. Some students who are planning to return to home countries may not be interested in extensive study of US culture.

Yet assignments—particularly in the humanities and social sciences— may assume that students know about US politics, history, or common cultural activities. References to commercials, books, films, celebrities, political scandals, or fashion trends may be out of reach, even for domestic students whose home culture is not white, suburban, or middle class. Students may feel alienated by hearing these references with no explanation, but this becomes even more problematic if students are required to employ cultural knowledge that they don't have in order to complete an assignment. For instance, US writing classes often ask students to analyze advertisements but international students may not be able to identify the subtle cultural messages operating in many ads. A Latinx student may be able to demonstrate the deepest knowledge of a Spanish-language commercial; however, the instructor may be incapable of understanding that commercial. Both situations place some students at a distinct disadvantage.

If assignments do assume cultural knowledge, then ask how the cultural knowledge functions within the assignment and how that assignment functions within the curriculum and course goals. If cultural knowledge is merely an engaging context, then consider creating a different, more global context or multiple contexts that can appeal to more student populations. If the cultural knowledge is essential to the assignment and curriculum, look for ways to make the assignment accessible for all students. At a minimum, faculty should provide important explanations to students who need it. Faculty might also modify the original assignment or create an alternative assignment. For example, in the advertisement assignment above, students might analyze an ad from a home culture, providing translation as needed. Or, the teacher might create additional conferences with multilingual students in order to identify and explain an ad's cultural messages.

In the *Case Study* below, Nicole Reynolds shares how she scaffolds her formal writing assignments for students with diverse backgrounds, both linguistic and disciplinary.

CASE STUDY: PREPARING STUDENTS FOR THE GRADUATE SEMINAR PAPER

Students in my Women's, Gender, and Sexuality Studies (WGSS) graduate seminars—international and domestic—come from a variety of fields. Styles and genres of writing can differ dramatically from field to field. Some students in my seminar are pursuing the graduate certificate of achievement in WGSS, but many others are not; the level of familiarity with feminist texts, theories, and practices can vary widely.

I hold a joint appointment in English and WGSS. In my courses for both programs, having students talk and write about what they've read are the ways I gauge the extent to which they've grappled with course material. In the humanities, a seminar paper and the exercises that lead up to it (proposal and annotated bibliography) constitute a typical summative project for a graduate seminar. I've found that these formats— or the ways that these formats are utilized in the humanities—can be overwhelmingly unfamiliar to graduate students whose expertise is in very different areas. In many ways, this levels the playing field between international and domestic students: perceived advantages of being a native English speaker balance out when some or nearly all are starting from scratch, or nearly so, to adapt the language, research methods and genres of a new discipline (WGSS)—or of a familiar discipline but from a new scholarly perspective (humanist)—and at an advanced level.

I've found it very important to recognize and to articulate concretely the elements of an assignment that are based in the (often unarticulated) givens or assumptions of a specific discipline or of US academic culture more generally. Sometimes this can amount to a crash course in standards and practices of graduate-level research and writing. Given the interdisciplinary nature of WGSS, and the varied levels and types of training graduate students bring to the courses, such a review proves beneficial to international and domestic students alike. For example, I provide an overview of our library's resources in WGSS. I distribute and discuss descriptions of 1) what it means to write in the humanities, 2) how to frame and "pitch" an argument in an essay proposal, and 3) the graduate seminar paper: its objectives, general structure, and stages of development. Together with 4) a detailed discussion and examples of annotated bibliographies, I review the differences between paraphrase and summary, discuss when and how to use direct quotation, and study the difference between an author's abstract of his or her article and a reader's summary and evaluation (annotation) of that article. Students receive feedback from me after each assignment, so that as they work toward the final product (the seminar paper) they have steady input on the progress of their research (the bibliography), the development of their thinking (from proposal to essay), and the revision of their writing (through multiple versions of their prose across these various components of the essay). Ideally, students will bring enhanced writing skills (and a dose of feminist theory!) to projects in their primary disciplines.

Dr. Nicole Reynolds
Associate Professor of English and Women's,
Gender, and Sexuality Studies
Ohio University

"How can I scaffold my writing assignments to help students be more successful?"

Students are more likely to be successful if lengthy or high-stakes writing projects are scaffolded in some way, or if assignments build upon one another or are broken down into more manageable chunks, as Nicole Reynolds describes above.

Asking students to draft their projects in advance is a common way to scaffold. Drafting minimizes a student's ability to wait until the last minute to begin a project as well as the possibility that the project is inappropriate for the assignment. Faculty might ask students to brainstorm ideas (or engage in one of the other informal activities above) and discuss them with a partner and then complete a peer review of a full draft. Or, students might submit a full draft to the instructor and receive feedback or participate in a conference. (For more on peer review and conferencing, see Chapter 7.)

It's often well worth instructional time to have students write a short proposal for your approval. A proposal can be as simple as a paragraph or one-page overview of the student's topic, argument, and the main points they are planning to pursue. The proposal can be assigned as homework or written in a few minutes of class time. Asking students to submit some kind of proposal can help redirect students who are substantially off topic or who have chosen a topic that is unlikely to be successful. By redirecting students early, we increase the chances that students will invest time on a worthwhile project.

Annotated bibliographies are another common scaffolding activity. Submitting an annotated bibliography means that students must choose a topic, identify sources, and begin reading well in advance of the deadline. As with a proposal, the annotated bibliography minimizes procrastination and gives faculty a chance to redirect students or to point them toward more useful source texts.

Students might also be required to submit large or complicated writing projects in sections. To use the traditional social science research paper as an example, students might submit an introduction and literature review first, then submit a methodology section a few weeks later, followed by the results and analysis, and conclude by submitting the entire paper with all sections revised.

Teachers can respond to drafts over email, with audio comments, through peer groups, or quickly as a whole-class activity. Although responding in front of the class obviously takes valuable class time, it involves less of the instructor's total time and generates synergy as one student's proposal sparks ideas for another student or allows the instructor to identify problematic patterns or misunderstandings. It can also teach students better questions to ask about their projects.

Beyond their pedagogical value, all of these scaffolding activities also help to minimize plagiarism. When students are responsible for generating multiple components or drafts of a paper for different deadlines, they are far less likely to wait until the last minute and then either cheat or paraphrase poorly.

"How can I employ text-matching software thoughtfully and strategically?"

Text-matching software or "plagiarism checkers" have limited utility, but utility nonetheless. The "reports" themselves, which usually offer some kind of matching index, are virtually useless. Some programs will identify all properly quoted text and accompanying citations as "matches." However, if faculty take the time to look at the matched text, the software reports do allow one to easily identify instances of blatant cheating, poor citation, and poor paraphrasing.

It is also useful to devote class time to discussing your expectations for textual borrowing since expectations vary between teachers and across disciplines. Take the time in class to discuss some of the scenarios in Workshop 6.1 or to compare some paraphrases with their original texts so that students are familiar with your expectations.

"How can I make assignments more plagiarism-resistant?"

1. Allow students to choose their own topics or choose among a range of topics.
Students are less likely to plagiarize if they are invested in their projects.

2. Ask students to submit their sources with their writing projects.
If you are really concerned about students' textual borrowing, then ask them to submit copies of their sources with borrowed material highlighted.

3. Watch for inconsistencies in students' papers.
Inconsistencies within a paper are a red flag that there are problems with textual borrowing. Do citation styles vary within the text? Is there a mix of American and British spellings? Is the writing in some sections of the text suddenly far stronger than the text as a whole?

4. Teach students how to keep good notes.
What strategies do you use to avoid plagiarism? Talk with some colleagues and collect a set of note-taking strategies that you can teach to students, like copying and pasting the reference and page number at the bottom of any note that you take.

"How can I use writing to develop a global perspective?"

There are a variety of ways to assess how students are developing as global citizens (see, e.g., Chapter 8). However, we suggest that writing projects are a particularly powerful tool for helping students to develop a global perspective. Asking students to write about their experiences challenges them to think about them more deeply and necessitates a processing of those experiences. Faculty might consider:

- Asking students to demonstrate some course-appropriate evidence of a global perspective through writing.
- Preparing students for a global encounter by having them complete a research paper, inquiry paper, or personal essay.
- Allowing students to process their experiences through a journal, personal essay, or memoir. All of these genres create a place to vent about experiences, process trauma or distress, and to see change in themselves. Personal essays or memoirs might ask students to reflect on those journal entries and focus in on particular aspects of their experiences or changes in perspective.
- Asking students to share what they've learned through photo or video essays, presentations, or websites.

 THE WORKSHOP

6.1 Identifying the Hidden Curriculum in My Writing Assignments

Choose one of your regular writing assignments (or perhaps one where students have often struggled or turned in weak work). After analyzing it yourself, you may also find it helpful to have peers analyze your assignment. They may be able to identify issues you've overlooked. Consider the following questions as you or a colleague analyze the assignment:

- What are my goals for this assignment? Why do I have students do this?
- What intellectual tasks does this assignment ask students to engage in?
- What political acts does this assignment ask students to engage in?
- What cultural knowledge does this assignment assume?
- How might someone from outside the United States understand this assignment?

- How might someone from a minority culture within the United States understand this assignment?
- How might this assignment be modified so that it is more accessible to multilingual and other diverse students? Or, what alternate assignment could achieve the same goals?
- What resources can I provide to help multilingual writers understand the intellectual tasks and cultural knowledge?

6.2 Defining Poor Textual Borrowing

As we described earlier, defining plagiarism or poor textual borrowing is easier said than done. Consider how you would respond to the scenarios below and discuss with a partner, if available. You might even share them with your classes in order to talk through the range of definitions operating in your classroom. This kind of open discussion can help students meet *your* expectations regarding textual borrowing as well as help them to understand that other faculty may have very different views on the same scenario.

a) Amy's instructor reads her paper and notices a few sentences that seem suspicious. They certainly don't sound like Amy's writing, but there are no quotation marks. Later in the paper, the instructor finds quoted material, but no attribution to a particular author or she finds an author, but no page number. She also finds spots where Amy discusses a particular source that doesn't appear in Amy's bibliography. What should she do?

b) Asmina is working on a history paper about William Wilberforce. Two different sources talk about his childhood in Hull. When she writes her paper, Asmina writes that "William Wilberforce was born and raised in Hull." She doesn't give a citation because she knows this fact is common knowledge. But is it? What constitutes common knowledge in your field?

c) Last term, Mia wrote a paper on Myanmar for her Southeast Asian Studies class. This term, she is asked to write another paper for her history class. She thinks that last term's paper on Myanmar fits this new history assignment pretty well. Can she turn in her Myanmar paper again for her history class?

d) Xilin is an international student who is struggling with understanding his sources for his paper. He knows that he needs to paraphrase, but he doesn't understand his sources well enough to do a good job. He changes a few words here and a few words there because he has been told that as long as he changes every other word that he is paraphrasing. What advice would you give Xilin?

e) Viktor is working on a conference presentation. He will be presenting on some of his research that came out in a journal last month. While creating his slideshow, Viktor copies and pastes several quotes from his article. He doesn't mention that they appear in his journal article. Has Viktor plagiarized him*self* by copying his own words?

f) Juan and Yoko have been working together on research for several months and recently wrote up the results in a report for their advisor. Now Juan is writing his dissertation. He needs to write about the research he and Yoko worked on last year. He pastes several pages of the earlier report into his dissertation with no citation. Has he plagiarized? What if he had noted that the pasted text was co-authored by Yoko?

g) Jia was doing research with the help of his advisor. When the project was finished, Jia wrote up the results for his advisor. Portions of Jia's text later appear in one of the advisor's published papers, but Jia has not been listed as a co-author or consulted about the text. Now Jia needs to include those same results in his thesis. Does he need to cite his advisor's paper, even though Jia did the original writing? If he doesn't cite the advisor's paper, has he then plagiarized? Or has the advisor plagiarized Jia's work?

h) Jerry is busy writing his dissertation. He needs to describe the procedure he used in his experiment, which includes how he operated the lab equipment. The instructions for the equipment's use are pasted to the machine. Should he try to paraphrase the instructions? If he does, couldn't he misrepresent the way the machine is operated? But if he copies the instructions word for word, how is he supposed to quote or cite the operating instructions?

6.3 Making Your Assignments Plagiarism-Resistant

We don't deny that there are some students who set out to cheat; however, in some cases, we also make it really easy for them to do so. When we give students boilerplate assignments, we're more likely to get boilerplate in return. This is particularly true when we ask all students in the class to work with the same text in the same way (e.g., "Write a book review of [insert popular text that hundreds of people have written about online here]"). Jessica Hollis describes how she made an assignment more plagiarism-resistant in the *Case Study* that follows.

Take one of your current writing assignments and evaluate its plagiarism-resistance. Consider:

a) Does this assignment require students to include some personal element? A personal element makes it harder to find/buy an existing paper that matches the assignment. Asking students to include a limited personal element may have other learning benefits as well. You might ask students to write a brief reflection on the writing process, write a cover letter requesting feedback on particular questions, narrate their research processes, or include an element of personal critique or evaluation.

b) Is the assignment scaffolded? Asking students to submit a proposal, an annotated bibliography, a rough draft (or all of the above) encourages students to get started on a project earlier. Scaffolding thereby mitigates the procrastination that sometimes leads students to cheat.

c) How can the core of the assignment be made more specific? Generic tasks (e.g., write a book review) of common texts make it easy for students to share or buy papers or to engage in substantial copy-and-paste work. Can you ask students to take a particular point of view, use a specific theoretical or methodological lens, or ask them to put two texts in conversation with each other? Or to employ some element from class? Or to engage in two tasks instead of one (e.g., write an analysis and critique)?

d) Revise your assignment, working to make the assignment more specific, add a personal element, and incorporate at least some scaffolding. Share the revised assignment with a few colleagues to see whether they have additional ideas for making it plagiarism-resistant.

CASE STUDY: CIRCUMVENTING PLAGIARISM CREATIVELY

When I started teaching the Western (think John Wayne, cowboys) a couple of years ago in my junior-level writing course, I imagined I had made reading and assignment choices that would go far in both making the material more accessible to international students and circumventing plagiarism among all students. I taught short stories but stories that little or nothing had been written about; thus, students could not seek out other sources to "help" them write about these stories. Likewise, I required specific sources for use in these writing assignments, creating a more supervised incorporation of "research" sources.

While such strategies did prevent plagiarism and allowed me to teach students something about what plagiarism is and how to avoid it, the writing itself didn't tend to be very insightful or engaging. Moreover, when it came to talking about writing (or even writing about it), the one or two international students were reluctant to participate. The kind of writing I was asking them to do—critical analysis where they had to make a point of their own about a story—was simply not a form they were comfortable with.

Subsequently, I have incorporated a more creative assignment to address this challenge. Since part of the course focuses on film, I have students create their own Western scene. They imagine a scene they would like to film, describe how they would film it, discuss what ideas they want the scene to address/explore, and explain how their choices accomplish this. Prior to the assignment, I introduce them to basic film terminology and techniques, and we analyze Westerns for how film techniques are employed to convey those ideas. Their writing assignment, then, is part creative and part analysis of their own creation.

This assignment has proven much more doable to all of my students, but especially my international students. They feel more comfortable writing about something visual, especially their own creation, and they participate more in workshops. They are more willing to respond substantially to comments about their own work and to ask questions about that of their classmates. My sense is that the visual and film technique elements of this assignment seem like a more universal language (even though, ironically, English is used to discuss them); language barriers may get in the way of how two people comprehend the written word, but we all see basically the same thing on the screen, even if we interpret it differently. Likewise, the technical film terminology is a textual language all students learn together going into the assignment.

When I first used this assignment, I placed it at the end of the term. I have subsequently assigned it earlier and earlier because it builds students' writing and speaking confidence as well as teaching them analytical skills that they then employ more adeptly when writing about other films and stories. This confidence in their own writing and analytical abilities in itself also helps circumvent plagiarism as we move through later assignments that require incorporating research sources: students feel more self assured of their own interpretations and do not feel the need to rely on (and are not overwhelmed by) the work of others.

Dr. Jessica Hollis
Assistant Professor of English
Ohio University

 ## DISCUSSION AND REFLECTION

1. What was the outcome of the assessments at the beginning of the chapter? Do you give students opportunities to develop as writers? Do you ask them to engage in a range of formal and informal writing to strengthen their writing

abilities? What about in your program's curriculum as a whole? Given your context, do you need to give writing a greater role in your classes?

2. What experiences have you had with students and poor textual borrowing? How have you responded in the past? Having worked through this chapter, would you respond to any of those situations differently?

3. When you examined your current writing assignments, did you identify any that disadvantage multilingual or other minority students? How did you decide to modify those assignments?

4. Did you identify current writing assignments where you are missing an opportunity to encourage students to think more globally? How did you decide to modify those assignments?

5. How did Jessica Hollis modify her writing assignment to make it more plagiarism-resistant? Could you adapt her ideas for your own context?

 BIBLIOGRAPHY

Adler-Kassner, L., & Wardle, E. (2016). *Naming what we know: Threshold concepts in writing.* Logan, UT: Utah State UP.

Bean, J. (2011). *Engaging ideas: The professor's guide to integrating writing, critical thinking, and active learning in the classroom* (2nd ed.). San Francisco, CA: Jossey-Bass.

Crusan, D. (2010). *Assessment in the second language writing classroom.* Ann Arbor, MI: University of Michigan Press.

Ferris, D., & Hedgcock, J. (2014). *Teaching L2 composition: Purpose, process, and practice* (3rd ed.). New York, NY: Routledge.

Howard, R. (1999). *Standing in the shadow of giants: Plagiarists, authors, collaborators.* Stamford, CT: Ablex.

Russell, D., & Foster, D. (2002). Rearticulating articulation. In D. Foster & D. Russell (Eds.), *Writing and learning in cross-national perspective: Transitions from secondary to higher education* (pp. 1–47). Mahwah, NJ: NCTE/Erlbaum.

Silva, T. (1993). Toward an understanding of the distinct nature of L2 writing: The ESL research and its implications. *TESOL Quarterly*, *27*(4), 657–677.

Part III

Assessment and Feedback

Chapter 7

Responding to Student Writing with a Global Perspective

 INTRODUCTION

Responding to student writing is time-consuming, challenging work. Moreover, it may feel fruitless when students don't make the recommended changes and improvements. Yet those moments when we see real student growth in writing are incredibly rewarding. In this chapter, we focus on structuring feedback so that students actually want to implement it.

While most chapters can be read independently, this one really does build upon the previous chapter. Having laid the groundwork of designing writing assignments that encompass and facilitate a global perspective, here we focus on what happens after the papers are submitted. As faculty, how can we respond to student writing in meaningful ways that encourage deep revision? How can we respond in ways that are not unduly time-consuming? How can we respond with a global perspective that is inclusive of diverse students?

By the end of this chapter, you should be able to:

- articulate and implement effective strategies for responding to global (big-picture) problems in students' writing;
- articulate and implement effective methods for responding to sentence-level problems in students' writing;
- adapt response strategies for multilingual writers;
- distinguish between corrective, directive, evaluative, and facilitative feedback;
- implement a toolkit of early interventions/early response practices to student texts; and
- develop activities that ask students to respond to each other's work.

CLASSROOM AND SELF-ASSESSMENT

As you begin this chapter, take a moment to reflect on your current response and grading practices. These assessments ask you to examine both your own practices and the practices you encourage within your students.

 ### ASSESSING MY STUDENTS' REACTION TO GRADED WRITING

In this chapter, you'll explore activities and strategies for responding to students' writing; however, it's useful to begin by thinking through your current practices. When students receive their graded papers, how do they typically react? How do you encourage students to revise?

Which of the following best describes your students' reaction to their graded, formal writing projects? My students usually:

0	complain that they don't understand my comments and/or that they don't understand the reason for their grades.
★	do nothing.
★ ★	make a few minor changes to their texts (e.g., proofread more carefully) and make a recognizable (though not necessarily successful) effort at one or two of the more substantive suggestions.
★ ★ ★	make substantial, successful revisions and tell me that my comments were helpful.

 ### ASSESSING MY OWN WRITING RESPONSE PRACTICES

Which of the following best describes your practices of responding to a student's formal writing project (e.g., term paper)? I typically write a letter grade or score and:

★	do nothing else.
★ ★	mark all (or many) sentence-level mistakes (in grammar, punctuation, citation style, etc.).

★★★	make a few summary comments describing big problems and note patterns of sentence-level mistakes.
★★★★	make substantial summary comments about major strengths and weaknesses while also making original, text-specific comments that engage with the writer's ideas. I also identify patterns of sentence-level mistakes.

ASSESSING HOW I ENCOURAGE STUDENTS TO REVISE THEIR WORK

Which of the following statements best describes your classroom practices? On most formal writing projects, my students:

★	submit one final draft, receive no comments, and have no opportunity to revise.
★★	receive some kind of feedback (either from me or from peers) before submitting a final draft OR they have an opportunity to revise to improve their grades.
★★★	receive feedback from me on a draft AND have at least one opportunity to revise based on my comments.
★★★★	receive feedback on a rough draft from me and from multiple peers. I provide substantial summary comments and marginal comments and then encourage students to revise.

KEY CONCEPTS

These *Key Concepts* focus on important scholarship that underlies effective response to student writing. We begin by raising awareness of rhetorical differences across cultures before highlighting types of response, ways of intervening in writers' texts before the final draft, and adapting response strategies for multilingual writers.

Rhetorical Differences across Cultures

Just as cultures have different preferences about communication (see Chapter 3), those preferences also carry over into writing, manifesting in differences in how arguments are made and genres are organized (Casanave, 2017; Connor, 2011). In the US academy, professors tend to prefer extremely direct, linear arguments that have a clear purpose/argument that has been previewed early in the text; however, this preference does not hold for other cultures.

Although it is easy to oversimplify or stereotype students' writing based on their cultures, it's still important to approach response with an awareness that rhetorical traditions and values do vary. In Chapter 6, Lana Oweidat mentioned her challenges with adapting from an Arabic rhetorical pattern to a US one. Many writers from other cultures face comparable challenges. In the *Student Voice* below, Amanda Hayes describes how she came to recognize that Appalachian culture privileged a different rhetorical structure than the one she was struggling to learn in school.

STUDENT VOICE: APPALACHIANS DON'T WANT TO TELL ANYONE "WHAT TO THINK"

I was pretty young when I learned that I was Appalachian, but it wasn't until college that I started to learn what that might mean.

I'd always known that I liked reading and writing, though that didn't mean they came easily in school. I sometimes did very well on papers, and sometimes did far less well, but I couldn't have told you why. All I knew was that some teachers liked the way I wrote while others didn't. So it was my love rather than a talent that led me to major in English. In retrospect, I can see where this love came from. One of my first literacy memories is of my mother reading from *Little House in the Big Woods* before bed and pointing out that the lives described in the book were probably pretty similar to what my own ancestors, who had lived on the same farmland I did, would have known in our own big woods. My grandparents had a complete set of encyclopedias that were given pride of place on their living room shelves and that seemed like the font of all wisdom when I was little. We would often flip through them together. I remember pressing flowers and leaves in the well-read copy of our county's local history. Everywhere I looked, writing intersected with my family's lives.

I learned from these experiences to value writing, but even beyond that, to value stories. My family used stories—in books and in person—to remember, to value, and to *understand* the world. The story of Laura Ingalls Wilder's childhood became a history lesson on my great-grandparents' lives; an uncle's story of watching the USS Shenandoah crash during a storm taught me about the combustive properties of electricity.

Yet, it took me a long time to realize how much this cultural value for stories influenced my writing. If I were analyzing a novel, I took my reader through the "story" of my thinking, telling them how I connected with particular elements in the book. If I was writing about a contemporary social issue, I explored where my ideas about the issue came from, what stories I knew or had heard that made me think about specific issues in specific ways. In other words, I approached writing as a way to tell my stories, something that felt natural to me.

What I didn't seem to do in my writing was argue. In fact, one of the greatest mysteries to me in academic writing was the thesis. I knew, theoretically, what a thesis statement was—the essay's main point, the *argument*, boiled down to a sentence and injected into the introduction. Yet even when I thought I had written thesis statements, I would be told I was being too vague, or timid, or that I waited too long to even state my thesis. (I would often start a paper by trying to explain— through anecdote—why I was discussing the topic at hand, something that seemed important to me but that necessarily pushed my "point" further into the paper.) This was, of course, assuming my audiences perceived *any* thesis. Plenty of teachers told me they simply didn't see an argument in my papers at all.

What I certainly lacked was a way to think about why conventional, thesis-driven academic argument was so hard for me. It wasn't until I was in college that I explained my thesis problem to another student, who was studying writing and rhetoric, and who was herself from the Appalachian region. She didn't find it strange that my writing was more narrative, more exploratory than argumentative. She told me, "They just don't get that you're Appalachian. We don't want to tell anyone what to think."

This statement has stayed with me because it was the first time someone showed me how to think of my written voice in cultural terms. I don't think it's any accident I'm far more comfortable telling a story to illustrate or explore my own thinking rather than telling you what yours should be. Even if I didn't use "ain't" or "y'all" or any other regional terminology in my writing—and many Appalachian writers don't—my culture was still spilling onto the page in ways neither I nor my academic readers understood. But it's worth understanding. Science is discovering that human beings respond to stories on a much deeper level than we've ever realized. We're also realizing how truly difficult it is to change minds through conventional argument. So who knows, maybe Appalachian-style narrative writing is something more of us will come to value. I have.

Dr. Amanda Hayes
Assistant Professor of English
Kent State University-Tuscarawas

Amanda Hayes makes a choice here to perform her argument, thereby helping readers understand what an Appalachian, narrative argument is instead of making a traditional, academic one. You can read more of her argument for the importance of Appalachian rhetorics in her forthcoming book, *The Politics of Appalachian Rhetoric*. To learn more about other cultures' rhetorical traditions, consider Cushman (2013), Kirkpatrick and Xu (2012), or Jackson II and Richardson (2003).

Essential Research on Teacher Response to Student Writing

After an awareness of possible cultural differences, the most important thing for faculty to know about feedback is that there is no conclusive evidence that correcting students' sentence-level errors leads students to make those errors less frequently over the long term (Casanave, 2017; Ferris & Hedgcock, 2014). Students are more likely to learn from feedback when faculty intervene in preliminary drafts by identifying patterns of errors (e.g., a few mistakes made repeatedly, like a misspelled word or incorrect punctuation), but not correcting them. This encourages students to focus on improving their most frequent errors before submitting final projects.

Research also shows that students can quickly become overwhelmed or discouraged by feedback, whether that feedback is corrections or comments (Ferris & Hedgcock, 2014; Sommers, 2013). Students may not understand the teacher's feedback (even comments intended to be positive), may be discouraged by negative comments, or may be overwhelmed by the sheer volume of comments (Ferris & Hedgcock, 2014). For example, Jorge in Sommers' (2012) video, is frustrated by teachers who have simply written "good" on his papers. Although faculty may feel obligated to provide extensive responses and to identify every problem and mistake, this is actually counterproductive; it's also incredibly time-consuming. Students are more likely to benefit and make changes when they receive limited, focused comments and have an opportunity to revise.

Types of Written Feedback

In considering what makes feedback valuable, it's useful to take a step back and consider the kinds of responses faculty give. Feedback falls into roughly four categories: *corrective*, *directive*, *evaluative*, and *facilitative* (Dartmouth Institute for Writing and Rhetoric, n.d.). Faculty make *corrective* responses by correcting spelling, punctuation, or citation errors. As mentioned earlier, the efficacy of corrective response to promote learning is inconclusive. Moreover, corrective response only gets at the surface of the text; it doesn't address the ideas, claims, strengths, and weaknesses of a paper. Corrective feedback is time-consuming and often ultimately functions as a crutch, allowing faculty to tell themselves that they've done a lot of grading without actually giving the writer much help. It also communicates to students that grammar and mechanics are the only things that matter when there may be far more important abilities that students need to develop.

The second category of response is *directive*, or telling the writer what to do, either by making changes for the writer (e.g., rewriting a phrase) or writing commands in the text (e.g., "Delete this paragraph." "Don't use this word."). Directive response plays an important role in providing feedback, but again, is often overused. When providing directive response, faculty must avoid the temptation to treat our preferences as the One Right Way. Doing so can be confusing, discouraging, and foster a false belief that there is only one way when multiple approaches can usually be successful.

Turning our preferences into commands also takes the authority for a writer's text and ideas away from them (Severino, 2009) and confuses students when one person's preferences differ from another's. This isn't to say that faculty shouldn't have preferences or ask students to adhere to them, but they should articulate them as preferences instead of issues of categorical "right" and "wrong."

The third category is *evaluative*. This includes giving a paper a grade or score as well as comments like "good," "wrong," and "awkward." While evaluative responses are usually clear to writers, the path forward often isn't. Writers are often confused about how to make a sentence less awkward. Some writers are even frustrated by positive evaluative comments because they don't understand how they were actually successful. It's typically more helpful to suggest alternatives or try to explain why something is ineffective.

Facilitative is the final response type. Facilitative response encourages writers to make substantial, meaningful changes to their texts by engaging with writers' ideas and asking questions to clarify them. In facilitative response, faculty talk to the writer as a reader, sharing things they enjoyed, things that confused them, and things that they disagreed with. Facilitative responses also ask writers questions about their texts and make them responsible for changes (instead of making those decisions for writers). In many cases, facilitative responses are then the most effective for encouraging student learning. Table 7.1 compares examples of the different kinds of responses. As you can see, it may take much more space and time to provide facilitative responses. For this reason, consider responding electronically in the student's document or by recording audio comments.

Table 7.1 Comparison of Response Types

Issue	Corrective	Directive	Evaluative	Facilitative
Word choice: "hillbilly"	~~hillbilly~~ "woman from Appalachia"	"Wrong word"	"Offensive!"	"'Hillbilly' is an offensive stereotype to people from Appalachia and other rural areas. What are you really trying to get at through this term? Are you trying to describe socioeconomic status? Race? Level of education? I encourage you to choose another term that will clarify your meaning for readers without offending."
Confusing sentence	[Teacher rewrites the sentence]	"Rephrase"	"Unclear"	"I'm really confused here. Do you mean X or Y or something else?"
No thesis	[Teacher adds in a thesis based on a best guess about the paper]	"Include your thesis"	"-5 points, no thesis"	"There doesn't seem to be a thesis or argument that's guiding your paper. As a reader, this makes me feel confused and a little annoyed because I don't know why I'm reading or where this paper is going. Based on what you've written here, it seems like you want to argue that..."
Ineffective organization	[Teacher draws arrow moving the paragraph to the previous page]	"Move this paragraph"	"Disorganized"	"This paragraph seems out of place and disconnected from what comes before and after. What about moving it onto the previous page where you're also talking about [X]?"

There are several modifications that faculty often need to make when responding to a multilingual writer's papers if the student is still learning English. Those modifications are shown below in *Classroom Strategies*.

 ## CLASSROOM STRATEGIES

"How can I respond to student writing before the final draft?"

There are a variety of ways to respond before a final draft is submitted. In Chapter 6, we discussed ways of providing early responses by scaffolding the writing process, especially through proposals or annotated bibliographies. Once that ground work is in place, individual student conferences are a valuable strategy.

Conferences are a highly effective tool for responding to student writing. There is no avoiding the reality that individual conferences take 10–30 minutes per student depending on: 1) the length of the assignment; 2) the teacher's experience with conferencing (i.e., reading and assessing papers quickly); and 3) the teacher's experience with that particular assignment. However, conferences pay extremely high dividends.

During the conference, faculty can read students' drafts and identify important problems while there is still time to address them. Students also have the chance to ask questions and clarify feedback. After conferences, students typically understand assignments better and write stronger papers that take less time to grade. Because faculty have already read a draft of the paper, they know what to expect and can grade more quickly. Faculty can also be more rigorous because students have already received feedback and the teacher has already addressed any misunderstandings; thus, faculty don't feel compelled to give a better grade out of guilt.

Conferences are valuable for native English-speaking students and those benefits are magnified for multilingual students, who are likely to struggle more with understanding the prompt and developing an appropriate argument. In addition, conferences can help faculty understand multilingual students' purpose and language so that faculty aren't guessing about writers' meanings. Clarifying the overall project and main points through a face-to-face conversation makes it much easier to understand and provide useful feedback on students' texts.

Faculty can also respond to drafts asynchronously over email, with a file-sharing service or through an audio file. Asynchronous feedback is clearly more convenient, but can easily become more time-consuming. Sometimes the text is difficult to understand without the student's input and so faculty spend a long time trying to untangle the writer's intentions. It can also take

157

more time to write out feedback than simply having a conversation with the writer. Further, the time pressure of having the next student waiting outside forces faculty to provide some feedback and move on instead of obsessing over one paper. Finally, the face-to-face conference means that the student is investing time as well and so is more likely to use the time effectively (e.g., come with questions, ask for clarifications, etc.) and then actually make revisions.

There are, nevertheless, benefits to asynchronous feedback and many free programs available to provide it. Asynchronous feedback encourages faculty to focus in on a few key areas for revision. Making a quick audio or video recording is often appreciated by students and also makes your voice and tone clear. In online courses, recorded feedback can also help build relationships between faculty and students and mitigate isolation.

"How can I encourage revision through peer response?"

Writers can also benefit by receiving feedback from their peers. These activities can happen in pairs, in small groups, or with the whole class responding to one or two students' papers in class (Titus, 2017). Peer response activities do require planning in order for them to be successful though. This is especially important for classes with multilingual writers, who may not have had peer response experiences before and may feel threatened by having to critique the work of their domestic peers. When students recognize that peer response doesn't focus on sentence-level mistakes, many will feel more confident.

1. Lay groundwork with students before peer response begins.

Students may have had frustrating peer response experiences in the past, either because the activity was poorly designed or because the peer did a poor job. In consequence, be sure to teach students why you use peer response and how they might benefit from it. Remind students that although it is *possible* that they won't receive useful feedback, they will still benefit by learning to analyze another's writing. Students also often report understanding an assignment more fully and getting new ideas through the process of reading another student's approach to the assignment.

2. Create a useful peer response activity.

You might ask students to answer questions about the writer's text based on the grading criteria, or to look for all of the strengths in the text and then all of the weaknesses. Or, ask students to write each other short letters that discuss some of these issues (See Workshop 7.2 for additional ideas). Encourage students to focus on big-picture concerns instead of sentence-level mistakes. Several example activities are provided in the appendices and in Elbow and Belanoff's (2000) *Sharing and Responding*.

3. Provide examples of strong peer responses from previous classes or model peer response in class first.

Also consider making the activity worth credit. If students are simply asked to "read someone else's paper and give them some feedback," then they are unlikely to produce something worthwhile.

"What other strategies can support student writers?"

1. Build a drafting process and scaffolding into your assignment.

If we simply assign a final paper in the syllabus and wait for students to turn them in on the last day of class, we will often be left reading sub-standard results. (Scaffolding ideas are described in Chapter 6.) At a minimum, you can encourage students to minimize procrastination by setting due dates for a draft that are at least a week before the final deadline and asking students to complete some kind of peer response process (outside of class if necessary) and grading them in an all-or-nothing manner (e.g., 20 points if you submit; 0 points if you don't).

2. Find out what kind of response the student prefers.

Students come to our classes with such a range of needs and goals. Some students know they aren't going to revise and others already know that they are easily overwhelmed by (from their perspective) excessive comments. Still others want detailed feedback at all levels of their writing. Teachers often become justifiably frustrated when they take the time to write comments that students seemingly ignore. Some of this frustration can be alleviated by clarifying what kind of response the student prefers before grading. Faculty might do this through class discussion or by asking students to write a brief cover letter that asks for feedback in certain areas. It can be as simple as asking students to place a sticky note or other mark on their papers if they want feedback. You could also ask students to note whether they prefer comments that explain the rationale for their grades or comments focused on improving future papers (e.g., "place the thesis earlier in the text"; "provide more forecasting"; "offer a conclusion that does more than reiterate the paper").

3. Intervene with the writing center.

Most campuses have tutors available to support writers with academic papers. In most cases, tutors will help writers to strengthen the foundations of their papers—argument, main points, organization, development—before helping them with punctuation, citation form, etc. Remind students that writing centers do not operate like the dry cleaner; writers will need to schedule time to meet with the tutor and do the work, not drop off a "bad" paper and come back to retrieve a "fixed" paper. Also, encourage writers to bring a copy of their assignment and any faculty feedback to the session. This can help tutors make a more accurate assessment of the writer's project. Many writing centers also provide classroom presentations that explain what happens in a tutoring session, how to schedule a session, etc.

4. Provide sample papers to teach genres while complicating students' desire for formulas.

Undergraduate students are asked to write in a variety of genres to meet the disciplinary conventions of a variety of fields, not to mention the idiosyncrasies of faculty. And while graduate students may have gained mastery over undergraduate genres, they have rarely had experience with many of the high-stakes writing projects they encounter in graduate school. Providing students with sample papers is an easy way to alleviate anxiety about a writing project and to clearly communicate your expectations for the project while teaching them about genre. Keep in mind, though, that students have a tendency to fixate on a sample paper and over-model it, believing that everything about that paper must be precisely what the professor wants since it was provided as a "model." It's therefore especially helpful to provide several sample papers that are more and less successful, do different things well, or approach the genre in different ways. By providing a range of samples and describing (either in class or through annotations on the paper) their strengths and weakness, we teach students that there are multiple successful ways to approach a writing project. We also teach them that the conventions of, for example, a critique, aren't completely rigid and vary somewhat based on the audience. Iris's experience in the *Case Study* below affirms the value of providing sample papers, but also suggests that we need to teach writers that the conventions of a genre vary depending on the writer's audience; there isn't "One Right Way."

CASE STUDY: THERE IS NO "ONE RIGHT WAY"

Sample papers are valuable tools to help writers understand assignment expectations. However, some writers can take the idea of a "model" paper too far. Iris was a successful multilingual graduate student who became so dependent on model papers and templates that she became paralyzed if they weren't provided. She routinely used models as a generating tool for writing projects, but she gave them so much authority that even after regularly earning high grades, she was essentially incapable of beginning a paper without having first seen a model.

This issue came to a head when Iris received an article review assignment in which the professor's assignment criteria conflicted with a model she had learned in another class. Iris (in Phillips, 2008) reported: "Dr. H gave us guidelines. [...] It's different from what I have learned.... I was taught first paragraph you need to say the main idea of this article review. For example, 'This article has two strengths and one weaknesses' and what they are and then we list the strengths and weaknesses in details...." Iris was seriously confused and somewhat distressed to find that Dr. H could have a different definition of an article analysis than she had learned before. She said, "I couldn't have thought about applications or implications [if the assignment hadn't explicitly asked for them]. [If the professor] didn't tell us these aspects, I would have written it in the way I was taught and I would have been in trouble...." This ultimately became a significant learning moment for Iris as she began to recognize that some genres are quite flexible and that faculty may define them differently.

Dr. Talinn Phillips
Associate Professor of English
Ohio University

Although Iris, as a multilingual student, may have been especially likely to give too much authority to a model paper, native English-speaking students are susceptible to this as well. Providing more detailed criteria (in contrast to simply "write an article analysis") and/or providing multiple sample papers are important to help students develop an understanding of genre and to meet your specific goals for an assignment.

"How should I choose among the types of response?"

In general, facilitative response is most effective for helping students revise a project, but there are certainly moments when the other types are needed. Also, be sure to respond to a range of issues instead of "only ideas" or "only grammar" (Ferris & Hedgcock, 2014, p. 241). Since facilitative response is a bit more time-consuming and takes much more space, use it:

- when it's important for writers to own their decisions;
- when you're genuinely confused about what the writer is trying to do;
- when there are multiple, valid paths forward;
- when you don't like what the writer has done, but it's a preference and not a mistake;
- when the writer needs to think more deeply or more carefully;
- when the writer needs to do a better job of inhabiting the audience's point of view.

Choose one of the other types of response:

- when the writer has ignored some key aspect of an assignment;
- when you think the writer is able to fix the problem with little or no explanation/suggestions from you;
- or, in contrast, when you think the writer won't be able to generate an alternative word or correct the spelling, etc. unless you give an example;
- when the problem is egregious and absolutely must be addressed;
- when you think the writer may be getting overwhelmed by facilitative comments;
- when giving writers advice for issues to address in future papers.

Also, when giving feedback to students, be sure that comments address the *What*, *Why*, and *How*. What is the issue? Why is it a problem? How might the writer address the problem?

"How can I adapt my response strategies for multilingual students?"

1. Uncover the hidden curriculum in your response.

Multilingual students may not understand cultural references, slang, or idioms in your comments. They may also struggle to understand abbreviated comments like "awk," etc. Work to be straightforward as you respond, both in choice of words and in distinguishing between true suggestions and veiled commands. Native

English speakers are more likely to be familiar with hedging moves teachers often make (e.g., "You might want to consider…"), couching our critiques and demands as suggestions. Multilingual students may not pick up on these subtleties and then be justifiably upset when penalized for not making a change they thought was optional.

2. Offer multilingual students additional opportunities for support.

Given that many multilingual students have had little previous writing instruction, provide additional conference and revision opportunities so that they receive adequate feedback. Or, consider assigning the project earlier in the semester and offering all students additional opportunities for feedback before the final draft is due.

3. Decide how you will handle sentence-level problems.

Many students struggle with sentence-level errors in their writing, especially multilingual writers and students with disabilities. These students are already doing more work than many of their peers as they learn a new language or manage a disability; thus, it is often inappropriate and counterproductive to penalize students harshly for minor errors that do not obscure meaning. In some cases, faculty simply need to work harder to read through students' errors to the underlying meaning. In other cases, errors can become catastrophic, making it impossible to understand the text. We share faculty members' concerns that weak writing may reflect poorly on institutions and that it may misrepresent students' abilities to employers, etc. and we discuss specific strategies for responding to error and helping students reduce error below. But as you work to manage the tension between ethics and standards, consider:

- Does our curriculum provide students with adequate opportunities to write in low-stakes or ungraded projects that will help them improve their writing and develop confidence?
- Does our curriculum teach students to plan, draft, and revise based on feedback?
- Is this a high-stakes project, like a grant or résumé that needs to be error-free, or is it a lower-stakes project where some error is not catastrophic?
- Do the errors obscure meaning or are they simply annoying? Focus on errors that obscure meaning and identify one or two patterns of error for the student to improve.
- Do the errors reveal a lack of vocabulary (which you can teach to writers during the writing process) or problems that are rule-governed (like verb tenses)? For rule-governed problems, encourage or require students to

keep an error log (Ferris & Hedgcock, 2014) and point students to web resources that can help them develop competence.

- Are sentences incorrect, or are they unusual expressions? If the language is technically correct, then ask whether there is a real problem or if the writer is being penalized for having a written accent.

"How can I help students reduce errors in their writing?"

1. Distinguish between issues of style and error.

Be mindful that there is a difference between error, personal preferences, and phrasing that is awkward or inappropriate in tone. Students can easily become confused and frustrated when we mark as mistakes phrasing that we just don't like or find somewhat inappropriate. Word choice and phrasing are very important because of their impact on tone and the writer's credibility, but this is a different kind of problem from a comma splice, which is completely rule-bound and simply wrong.

2. Explain the implications of writers' choices and offer alternatives.

It's certainly valuable to tell students when a word or phrase feels awkward or has a connotation that seems inappropriate or is too informal. However, instead of crossing out a word and replacing it without explanation, explain the issue and offer alternatives.

3. Teach self-editing strategies.

Encourage students to proofread more effectively. Strategies for effective self-editing include reading a paper aloud, proofreading for one kind of problem at a time, and working through the paper from back to front (to avoid skimming over/assuming the correct form and not seeing the mistake) (Ferris & Hedgcock, 2014).

4. Focus on patterns of error, not one-time mistakes or typos.

Most writers make a few mistakes over and over again and these patterns are the mistakes they are most likely to learn from. Also, writers are more likely to improve when they focus on a few mistakes instead of addressing a range of problems at once. Help writers focus on simple mistakes first (e.g., misspelled words or the wrong format for citations) and then work up to more complicated problems like comma usage or unusual verb tenses.

"How should I respond to sentence-level problems?"

1. Develop the discipline of reading through errors.

Most of us have spent years training ourselves to proofread our work carefully and take errors seriously. Even minor errors in a high-stakes document like a grant can be catastrophic. Students, however, are usually not writing high-stakes documents; in their writing, we often need to focus on the arguments they're making and the development of the work instead of on errors. This is especially true in early drafts, when the language may change substantially before the final version or students haven't yet focused on proofreading. Since we have trained ourselves to read carefully for errors, we then need to retrain ourselves to read *through* errors to focus on larger issues, or at least make sure we're responding to the *whole* paper and not just to error (Matsuda & Cox, 2009). Reading through error is a self-discipline that we develop with practice. As we learn to strategically ignore error, we get more skilled at understanding the real issues in a student's text.

2. Remember that "grammar" problems may be gaps in vocabulary.

Many of the grammar problems in student writing (especially multilingual students) are actually gaps in vocabulary. You can then teach students vocabulary that they might not know, especially the language of your field or other academic language, including "chunks" of words (collocations or sentence stems). A few examples include phrases like "As I have shown" or "underlying assumption," or "with the exception of." Students might have learned these phrases incompletely and thus make mistakes or use language that feels awkward. Teaching students these "chunks" of language instead of focusing on correcting errors can help them avoid mistakes and also help them sound more professional/academic. The Manchester Academic Phrasebank (www.phrasebank.manchester.ac.uk/) and Graff and Birkenstein's (2010) *They Say/I Say: The Moves That Matter in Academic Writing* are both excellent resources for learning academic vocabulary.

3. Remember that "grammar" problems may be a symptom of cognitive overload.

When students are mentally taxed from engaging with radically new content or from working in a new genre, established abilities like punctuation, citation systems, or grammar might falter while these new competencies are being developed (Bean, 2011). If a writing project is really stretching students into new learning, consider giving students a few minutes in class to proofread before submitting.

4. Remember that most multilingual writers will have a written accent.

Perfection is not a reasonable goal for most of us when using a second or additional language. Just as we recognize that non-native English speakers will have a spoken accent, most will also have a written accent. It's usually unproductive to mark mistakes in, for example, article and pronoun use.

5. When you notice problems, don't assume that you know what the writer meant.

While it's important to read through error, there are certainly moments when we just cannot uncover the meaning in a writer's text. When this happens, it's best to ask the writer to clarify. If you can't schedule a conference or meet after class, then identify the problem area clearly in the text and explain why you're confused, offering possible interpretations. In many cases, it's best to wait for the writer to clarify before responding to an early draft. Our guesses about students' intentions are often wrong, and then we waste time responding to the arguments we've invented for them instead of what they actually wanted to say.

"How can I encourage my students to engage in deep revision?"

1. Teach students about revision throughout the writing process.

Students may be most motivated to revise for a higher grade, but we can teach them about revision throughout our courses. Texts like Harris's (2017) *Rewriting* or Murray's (2003) *The Craft of Revision* and peer response activities teach the principle that writing is rewriting and provide activities for effective revision.

2. Encourage or require students to revise a final draft.

This can either be mandatory or incentivized by allowing students to earn a higher grade. Many students will graduate without ever learning that professionals rarely have the luxury of submitting a writing project once and walking away. Revision to comply with feedback is the rule; submitting a paper once is the exception. Allowing students to revise one or more significant writing projects during a course helps students learn to interpret and apply feedback, develop resilience, as well as deepen their learning on the paper's topic.

3. Develop a protocol for grading revised writing efficiently.

Although professors might feel daunted by the idea of grading a paper *again*, you can create a system that allows you to score revisions very quickly (i.e., 2–3 minutes depending on the length of the paper). Start by imposing strict deadlines and requirements that will encourage only committed students to complete a revision and then ask them to highlight the changes in the new draft. You might also tell students that you will only provide a score on the revision and not comments. Finally, consider asking students to provide a cover letter that includes your summary comments on the earlier version and how they have addressed those comments so that you can focus on problem areas instead of rereading the entire paper.

 THE WORKSHOP

7.1 Assessing Your Current Response Practices

Choose three or four examples of previous student work, trying to select an unsuccessful paper, a successful one, and a mediocre one. Examine and note important differences in how you responded to each.

- Did you spend a lot of time marking sentence-level problems? What patterns of error could you point out to these writers?
- Did you provide feedback on global or big-picture concerns like organization and development of ideas? If not, what feedback could you have provided to this writer?
- Evaluate the language that you used in your feedback. Do you tend to lean too heavily on corrective, directive, evaluative, or facilitative feedback? If there are few facilitative comments, then try revising comments to better communicate the "why" and suggest some alternatives. Identify important ideas in the text and converse with the writer through your comments and/or suggest issues to improve in future assignments.

7.2 Designing a Peer Response Activity

Which writing project do students struggle with most? Examine the sample peer response activities in Appendix A and create an activity for that project. In addition to the activity itself, consider the logistical elements below.

- How will you give students credit for their response work? What are the criteria for good peer response work?
- Will peer response take place in or out of class?
- Will you provide sample peer response work or model peer response in class?
- How will you organize the activity? Will students bring physical papers to class? Upload papers to a cloud-based class folder?

- Will you put students in groups, in pairs, or have the class do the activity together? Can students choose groups or will you assign them?
- How will students return feedback to the writer and submit it for credit?

7.3 Creating a Revision Policy

If you haven't allowed students to revise papers before, try creating a policy that you could incorporate into your class. The questions below will help you establish some parameters on revision since these choices make a substantial difference in the work that revision entails for you. What criteria are compatible with your class schedule, workload, and grading habits? Consider:

- Which writing projects can students use to revise? Any major project, or just one where students struggle most? Keep in mind that it can be difficult to respond quickly enough to papers at the end of the semester in time for students to revise effectively. You might move a due date forward by a week or not allow students to revise the last assignment.
- What makes students eligible for revision? Earning a low grade? Scheduling a conference with you or consulting a writing tutor? Writing a cover letter about how they've addressed your comments? Agreeing to address all comments? Placing a few limitations around revision eligibility creates a more meaningful opportunity for dedicated students and discourages less dedicated students from abusing your time.
- How will you encourage revision? Will you average grades together? Replace the grade? Provide bonus points? Is revision mandatory or optional?
- Will you allow students to revise a paper multiple times? Although many students won't take advantage of revisions, a minority will be interested in revising repeatedly to earn more points.
- When will the revision be due and how will students submit revised work?
- How will you respond to revisions? Will you make substantial comments, a few summary comments, or simply assign a grade?

 DISCUSSION AND REFLECTION

1. Early in this chapter, we noted that cultures don't just have preferred communication styles, but also preferred rhetorical patterns and styles. What do you value in an argument? Can you remember how that value was formed?

2. Amanda Hayes's *Case Study* highlights characteristics of Appalachian rhetoric. What do you know about other minority rhetorics that students might be bringing to your classes? Do you need to do some research?

3. How have you typically responded to student writing in the past? Have your previous response methods seemed to spark better writing?

4. Has your response to writing focused primarily on disciplinary content, attention to form (spelling, grammar, citation style), or writing development? What did you learn about your teaching through Workshop 7.1? Are there ways that you might need to rebalance your response practices?

5. What new response strategy or writing approach from this chapter seems most likely to be effective with your students? How will you tailor it to your own context?

APPENDIX A. SAMPLE PEER RESPONSE ACTIVITIES

Research Paper Peer Response

Remember that "yes or no" answers are not appropriate for peer response. Give the writer as much information as you can to help them revise.

1. Read through the assignment to remind yourself of the requirements for this paper.

2. Read through the paper and make comments as needed.

3. What is this paper's argument? Is it clear, interesting, and appropriately placed? If not, explain.

4. Is the tone appropriate? If not, identify problem areas and explain why you found them to be inappropriate.

5. Consider the writer's use of quotations in this paper. Are quotations underused? (If so, identify some places where quotations would strengthen the paper.) Are they overused? (If so, identify some places where the quotation is unnecessary.) Is the purpose and function of quotations clear to you?

6. What questions do you still have about this topic after reading the writer's paper?

7. What questions were answered for you by reading the paper?

8. Did the writer convince you? If so, how? If not, why not?

9. At the end of the writer's paper, write a half-page response summarizing the strengths of the paper and another half page that identifies key areas for revision.

Kinesthetic Peer Response

1. Bring a paper copy of your paper (print single-sided!), a pair of scissors, and an envelope to class.
2. Take your paper and use scissors to cut across the top, removing your name and the title into one strip.
3. Now cut each paragraph apart into individual paragraphs. If a paragraph extends onto another page, then use tape to join the paragraph together.
4. When you have cut the paper into individual paragraphs, mix them up thoroughly and place them in the envelope. Pass the envelope to a peer.
5. When you receive an envelope with another student's paper, read through the paragraphs and put them in the order that seems best to you. Return the reordered paragraphs to the writer.
6. When you receive your reordered paper back, compare your original organization with your peer's organization. Which do you prefer and why? If there are differences, ask your peer about why they chose the order that they did.

Says and Does Peer Response

This exercise is adapted from Elbow & Belanoff (1989, pp. 37–39). Read through the paper and do a "Says and Does" analysis using your word processor's commenting tool. For *each paragraph* of the paper, you will tell the writer what you think the paragraph "says" (e.g., "Tells me that Ebonics is an important issue for our schools…") and "does" (e.g., "provides the motivation for your paper"). **"Says" is a one-phrase or one-sentence summary of the paragraph; "does" is a one-phrase or one-sentence analysis of how the paragraph functions in the paper.** Examples of what a paragraph "does" include (but are not limited to):

- introduces topic,
- provides background information,
- identifies argument,
- gives evidence to support _____,
- argues that _____,
- gives reasons for _____,
- makes a connection between _____ and _____,
- sets up the reader for _____,
- identifies a problem,
- identifies a solution, and
- creates a possible future.

While you're doing your "says and does" analysis, feel free to make other comments on the paper, particularly if the writer made a really great point or if something is unclear, unsupported, etc.

BIBLIOGRAPHY

Bean, J. (2011). *Engaging ideas: The professor's guide to integrating writing, critical thinking, and active learning in the classroom* (2nd ed.). San Francisco, CA: Jossey-Bass.

Casanave, C. (2017). *Controversies in second language writing: Dilemmas and decisions in research and instruction* (2nd ed.). Ann Arbor, MI: University of Michigan Press.

Connor, U. (2011). Intercultural rhetoric in the writing classroom. Ann Arbor, MI: University of Michigan Press.

Cushman, E. (2013). *The Cherokee syllabary: Writing the people's perseverance.* Norman, OK: University of Oklahoma Press.

Dartmouth Institute for Writing and Rhetoric. (n.d.) Responding to problems: A facilitative approach. Retrieved from http://writing-speech.dartmouth.edu/learning/support-writing-research-and-composing-technology/staff/responding-problems-facilitative

Elbow, P., & Belanoff, P. (1989). *Sharing and responding.* New York, NY: Random House.

Elbow, P., & Belanoff, P. (2000). *Sharing and responding* (2nd ed.). Boston, MA: McGraw-Hill.

Ferris, D., & Hedgcock, J. (2014). *Teaching L2 composition: Purpose, process, and practice* (3rd ed.). New York, NY: Routledge.

Graff, G., & Birkenstein, C. (2010). *They say / I say: The moves that matter in academic writing.* New York, NY: W. W. Norton.

Harris, J. (2017). *Rewriting: How to do things with texts* (2nd ed.). Logan, UT: Utah State University Press.

Indiana University Plagiarism Test (www.indiana.edu/~academy/firstPrinciples/certificationTests/index.html) A thoughtful, nuanced online activity that teaches students to distinguish between effective and ineffective paraphrases without oversimplifying complexities. Editions available for either graduate or undergraduate students.

Jackson II, R., & Richardson, E. (2003). *Understanding African American rhetoric: Classical origins to contemporary innovations.* Ann Arbor, MI: Routledge.

Kirkpatrick, A., & Xu, Z. (2012). *Chinese rhetoric and writing: An introduction for language teachers.* Anderson, SC: Parlor.

Matsuda, P., & Cox, M. (2009). Reading an ESL writer's text. In S. Bruce & B. Rafoth (Eds.), *ESL writers: A guide for writing center tutors* (2nd ed., pp. 42–50). Portsmouth, NH: Boynton/Cook.

Murray, D. (2003). *The craft of revision* (5th ed.). Boston, MA: Cengage.

Phillips, T. (2008). *Examining bridges, expanding boundaries, imagining new identities: The writing center as bridge for second language graduate writers* (Unpublished doctoral dissertation). Ohio University, Athens, OH.

Purdue Online Writing Lab (https://owl.english.purdue.edu/owl/) Perhaps the most well respected online writing source, the OWL provides extensive, free resources for supporting writing and grammar development, and for following style guides such as MLA and APA.

171

Severino, C. (2009). Avoiding appropriation. In S. Bruce & B. Rafoth (Eds.), *ESL writers: A guide for writing center tutors* (2nd ed., pp. 51–65). Portsmouth, NH: Boynton/Cook.

Sommers, N. (2012). *Beyond the red ink.* Boston, MA: Bedford/St. Martin's. Available at: www.youtube.com/watch?v=PKfLRz7h7gs

Sommers, N. (2013). *Responding to student writing.* Boston, MA: Bedford/St. Martin's.

Titus, M. (2017). "I get to choose what I want to be done with my paper": Teacher revision pedagogy, student revising practices, and student agency. *Journal of Teaching Writing,* 32(3), 1–31.

Chapter 8

Assessment in the Global Classroom

 INTRODUCTION

This chapter discusses two aspects of assessment: designing inclusive and fair assessments that support students with diverse backgrounds and needs, and assessing global learning at the institutional and classroom levels. Assessment allows us to plan instruction, determine if an objective has been met, assign grades, and reflect on student learning as a whole; it can also allow institutions to exhibit their unique qualities and excellence (Suskie, 2018) and provide information to students as they plan and manage their learning. Ideally, assessment should be used to "structure educational environments so as to maximize talent development" (Astin & Antonio, 2012, p. 18). Demonstrating excellence, however, is not a given—careful planning based on clear goals is required, and few institutions sufficiently and systematically assess to what extent students are achieving the promised outcomes. An institutional commitment to assessment is crucial, representing an "intellectual curiosity about what and how well our students learn" and providing the means for developing "a sustainable culture of inquiry about students' learning" (Maki, 2010, p. 3). Assessing global learning is more meaningful when the institution has a mission that explicitly includes and defines key terms (e.g., global learning) and has leadership that is empowered to advocate for programs and professional development. An often overlooked component of that commitment is the feedback students receive, as it has the potential to (but does not necessarily) contribute greatly to student learning. Building on foundational concepts related to fair and inclusive assessments, in this chapter we provide practical strategies from the institutional to the classroom level, and outline options for quantitatively and qualitatively assessing progress toward global learning goals.

By the end of this chapter, you should be able to:

- reflect on how students' backgrounds can affect their performance in unanticipated ways on your assessments;
- identify and discuss factors to consider and strategies to try in order to increase the likelihood that you are assessing diverse student populations fairly and providing useful feedback; and
- identify options to assess global learning at the institutional and classroom levels.

CLASSROOM AND SELF-ASSESSMENT

Before reading about *Key Concepts* and identifying specific strategies you can use, take a moment to reflect on your situation by rating to what degree your course assessments are inclusive and support students from diverse backgrounds and learning styles. See the Preface for tips on assessing students' knowledge and values.

ASSESSING TO WHAT EXTENT YOUR ASSESSMENTS ARE INCLUSIVE AND SUPPORT DIVERSE LEARNERS

Assessments of student work can be inspirational, providing evidence of learning and accomplishments, or they can seem to unforgivingly showcase gaps in students' knowledge. While low grades can occur due to student disinterest, time mismanagement, or under-preparation, poor performance can also be the result of the assessments themselves. As an educator, how well do you think your assessments support the many types of learners in your classes? Do you try to create at least some assessments that may be more inviting to potentially marginalized students? Do you try to make grading criteria as clear as possible?

My assessments are designed so that:

★	they are not based on authentic tasks or criteria; expectations are not fully transparent and clear; students from diverse backgrounds have no opportunity to utilize their experiences; students are not given opportunities to be involved in evaluating their own learning; there are few assessments and students receive minimal feedback.
★ ★	they are not fully based on authentic tasks or criteria; students from diverse backgrounds have limited opportunities to utilize their own backgrounds; students are given few opportunities to be involved in evaluating their own learning; there is some variety in assessment types and students receive at least some feedback.

	they are based on authentic tasks or criteria and have transparent expectations; students from diverse backgrounds have opportunities to utilize their own backgrounds and are encouraged to do so; students are involved in evaluating their own learning; there are smaller and larger assessments and students receive clear and sufficient feedback, often with a rubric.
★ ★ ★	

Example of a faculty member at the three-star level: A faculty member asks students to set learning goals at the beginning of the term and asks them to reflect on those goals periodically throughout the course. Before an exam, students are given sample test items for review, and actual test questions ask students to tie course concepts to experiences from their own lives. Small and ongoing assessments are utilized as well, including analyses of case studies and self-graded quizzes.

The remaining sections in this chapter provide background information on ways to reflect on course assessments and the degree to which they are fair for a variety of types of students, as well as discuss mechanisms to assess global learning.

 ## KEY CONCEPTS

Assessment in the global classroom is challenging. It requires not only careful planning, but also an awareness of a variety of students' needs and preparedness. A standard definition rightly prioritizes organization to inform student learning, such as this one by Walvoord (2010): "the systematic collection of information about student learning, using the time, knowledge, expertise, and resources available, in order to inform decisions that affect student learning" (p. 2). This definition, however, lacks an explicit awareness of the needs that diverse student populations may bring to the class. Not only is there the potential for instructor bias, but students who are less familiar with Anglo-Western educational norms may also be less able to demonstrate what they know or may be less familiar with culture-based references. In a global classroom, providing equitable assessments, or using methods most appropriate to the student is often more appropriate and fair than assessing diverse populations using identical methods and content, which can be biased toward specific groups. This section begins with a discussion on designing assessments that are inclusive and fair, including the topics of grading and feedback, and concludes with assessing global learning at the institutional and classroom levels.

Inclusive Assessment

The concept of *inclusive assessment*, which builds on more traditional definitions and stresses the reality of modern classrooms, can be defined as "a fair way of assessing

175

for learning that achieves the objective of measuring the learning outcomes of a course and awarding grades, while recognising student diversity and different learning styles" (Waterfield & West, 2010, p. 12). Enabling students to demonstrate their work to their full potential is thus the core of inclusive and equitable assessment. Assessment practices should also be relevant to students' futures outside of higher education (Boud & Falchikov, 2006). This goal of assessment, to not only aid students in meeting current course goals but also to guide their learning throughout their lives, is an important one for faculty striving to support their students as they develop as global citizens.

An inclusive assessment plan is based on learning objectives and begins with considering "what kinds of methods or tasks prompt students to represent the learning described in outcome statements" (Maki, 2010, p. 162); this includes providing opportunities for students to connect their prior experiences and background knowledge to the assessment (Ryan, 2005). Utilizing multiple assessment methods (e.g., oral, written, hands-on) is recommended, as this provides a more comprehensive picture of student learning with potentially less instructor bias. It's also important to take multiple data points on students' higher-order thinking skills while giving multiple opportunities for students to receive feedback. Assessments should capitalize on students' learning styles, and encourage them to reflect on their learning over time (Maki, 2010). Online intercultural exchanges can be assessed through evaluating participation engagement (Hauck & MacKinnon, 2016).

Fair and Equitable Formative and Summative Assessment

Assessments can move beyond exams or papers and can occur as an in-process evaluation for the purpose of informing instruction (formative assessment) or at the conclusion of an instructional period for the purpose of evaluating learning or achievement, for example to assign grades (summative assessment). It is generally easier to assess skills (which can be observed through behaviors) than to try to assess understanding.

Deciding on a specific in-class formative assessment can be challenging, given the many options and classroom realities (e.g., large classes, time restrictions, ranges in background knowledge). Educators can choose from four types: assessments of declarative learning (facts, principles); procedural learning (how to do something); conditional learning (when and where to apply knowledge or skills); and reflective learning (analyzing, synthesizing, evaluating, tying actions to beliefs) (Nilson, 2016). Nilson (2016) provides examples that can be useful for diverse classrooms. A formative assessment that is useful for both declarative and reflective learning is a background knowledge probe, in which students are asked questions (open-ended or multiple-choice) about their prior knowledge and also their beliefs or misconceptions about the subject matter. These questions can serve to activate background knowledge and guide instruction and can be structured to ensure that all students can feel included and supported. Technology can be useful, for example with online polling software, in order to show answers to stimulate discussion or for large classes. Another type of formative assessment is the application card, where students write down a real-world application of the course material (e.g., video, reading, speaker); responses can be shared with the class as appropriate. Other low-stakes, in-class techniques include self-graded quizzes, group problem-solving activities, brainstorming or freewriting, and periodic free-recall, where students share with a partner notes they've jotted down regarding important points and questions about lectures. This evidence of student learning can be used to determine to what degree students are meeting course goals, and if necessary, action can be taken to revise activities in order to improve student learning (Walvoord, 2010). Low-stakes formative assessment also allows students to monitor their own progress and identify areas for review.

It can be challenging to create summative assessments that allow diverse students to perform at their best. Final exams should be written with different types of students in mind, making expectations and content explicit and being mindful of the time it may take for some students to complete the exam during class. To reduce bias, blind grading (e.g., covering student names, using numerical identifiers, using anonymous online grading) can be used. Faculty can also check that the grades they've given haven't been influenced by writing style or by non-assessed components such as class performance (Driscoll & Wood, 2007). A portfolio or e-portfolio, in which a student gathers their work (e.g., written assignments, videos of discussions or presentations, reflection papers), can encourage reflection and demonstrate learning over time. Capstone projects can be structured to link academic study to future careers or the world, culminating in a final product, presentation, or performance. Final progress is more likely to reliably demonstrate student learning when students have access to examples and opportunities for low-stakes practice. Information gained from assessments can be used to plan for the rest of the course (formative), or to plan future courses (summative). Grading and feedback plays an important role in this process.

Grading and Feedback in a Diverse Classroom

In grading and providing feedback in a way that is most inclusive, a first consideration is often between giving norm-referenced vs. criterion-referenced assessments. With norm-referenced grading, student work is compared against classmates' work or achievement (often referred to as grading on a curve), while with criterion-referenced assessment, student work is compared against preset criteria or standards. In a criterion-referenced assessment, all students could conceivably earn A grades, as long as they meet the stated criteria. With norm-referenced, only the top scores earn the top grades. If norm-referenced grading is used, care should be taken to ensure that peer collaboration is prioritized over competition in the class, and that items didn't penalize students who were less familiar with cultural traditions or knowledge that was integral to the assessment. Whichever system is chosen, assessment expectations and policies should be made explicit and be based on stated criteria over mastery of academic discourse (Ryan, 2005). Asking colleagues or former students to review an assessment for potential bias can help minimize potential inequities (Suskie, 2018).

Students will benefit most from the grading process if they receive feedback that not only allows them to understand their grade, but also helps them for future learning. Formative feedback, for example, can be used with larger projects to motivate students earlier in the assessment and learning process. Comments should be timely and specific enough to guide students toward successfully meeting learning objectives (Nilson, 2016). Peer review and self-assessments allow students to create goals and periodically reflect on progress. Learning contracts allow students, working with the instructor, to write their own objectives, assignments, and due dates, with their work being evaluated according to the contract guidelines. Feedback can be delivered in various forms, such as through audio recordings. These processes can reduce the potential for bias in assessment. Scheduling time in class for students to review their grade and feedback allows them to ask questions. Students benefit from being told how they'll receive feedback and possible samples prior to having their first assignments graded. Feedback can be meaningful and have a great impact on student learning, or can be a source of frustration and lead to lowered self-confidence.

This *Case Study* from a student from a rural and lower socioeconomic area showcases the importance of understanding where students are coming from and how we can motivate them with our feedback.

STUDENT VOICE: STRUGGLING TO MEET UNIVERSITY EXPECTATIONS

My high school district was poor. We didn't have many options for courses, and teachers didn't have the luxury to specialize. I did very well in my school, though—a model student. In my French class, for example, I scored so well so consistently that my teacher stopped including my score in the test curve. But then I went to college.

I immediately realized that my professors taught much faster than the teachers I had in high school. And I wasn't prepared. Though I had studied French for three years and had over a 100% cumulative grade each semester, I tested into the second half of the beginner level of college French. How was that possible? I realized that my three years of French had covered the same material that should have been taught in one year. It was disheartening. I was afraid to talk to my professor about it, as I assumed that this was just how college classes were compared to high school classes, and that I would just have to catch up.

I did not continue to overachieve in my college French classes. I felt overwhelmed, and as the material got more difficult, I became less and less willing to volunteer in class, feeling like a fraud who did not belong, but also determined to pass the class. Increasing anxiety levels meant I had a harder time retaining information.

By the time I entered major level courses as a junior, my classmates were freshmen. They had apparently attended high schools that were more able to prepare students for university study. Only a few weeks into the semester, I went to talk to my professor and broke down crying. My professor kindly gave me some suggestions on how to organize my time, like setting daily goals for myself and dedicating specific windows of time to reading the assignments, which helped, but I was still on edge. I wish I had known then what I know now about how to learn. But I did not know the strategies that I could use to facilitate my own learning, and they weren't taught to me in high school or college. I started to shut down—when I made a mistake, I would spend the rest of the class thinking about it, red-faced and upset, not able to concentrate on what was being said.

This was when I finally recognized that maybe my experience in high school was not typical, and that this was not just the difference between high school and college-level coursework. I wish somebody had told me that. I came from a bubble of limited experience and had no frame of reference for the experiences of others. It would have helped if I at least understood why I was having problems, rather than not wanting to ask for fear that I would be seen as someone who was unprepared. I think it would have helped me for my professors in those early classes to get to know what backgrounds we were coming from and address any concerns that we might have. That support could have given me hope—I would not have felt so alone.

Though I stuck with the program, I never did catch up to my classmates. And trying to catch up in one class often means losing ground in others. There were times when I felt slightly abandoned, as though my professors had just given up on me, assuming that I was not willing to learn. This only increased my anxiety, as I felt pressured to prove myself not only to myself and my classmates, but my professors as well. But this pressure just slowed me down. I wanted to speak and I wanted to participate. I just did not know how.

On the day before I graduated, I was talking in English to one of my professors, who said, "You know, you're pretty good at speaking in French. I don't know why you don't talk more in class." I wish someone had told me this sooner. I wish things that I did well had been pointed out to me, because I couldn't see them. All I could see were my failures, and everyone else's successes. Assignments, participation, grading had all turned into anxiety and shame for me. What a difference four years makes.

Anonymous

BA in French and Linguistics, MA in Linguistics

This example showcases the role of background for many of our students, providing insight into how they might feel as their grades plummet though they strive so hard to succeed. Many universities do offer support services, yet not all students know how to access them or feel comfortable making the first move. As faculty, we can identify students who need additional assistance and also provide ongoing, constructive support and feedback.

Utilizing and Developing Rubrics

Rubrics are a common means of providing clear feedback with minimum instructor grading time. They outline criteria and levels of performance for student work and can be customized for any type of assignment. Many instructors find them useful for articulating and clearly sharing assignment objectives with students. They can also increase fairness, help faculty save time and refine their teaching skills, and help students focus on feedback and think critically (Stevens & Levi, 2012). Scoring can be calibrated between instructors for consistency and to reveal potential bias. They can be created collaboratively with students, and students can also be asked to assess their work with the rubric prior to turning it in for grading.

For global classrooms, careful consideration should be given to the criteria descriptors used (i.e., the left side of rubric) and to the explanatory comments for each performance level in order to increase the likelihood that students will understand expectations and feel included in the assignment. The weighting of the criteria should be considered as well so that students are not unfairly or unintentionally penalized. Online rubric generator samples (e.g., iRubric, QuickRubric, or Rubistar) should be evaluated prior to use to ensure they apply to students' backgrounds and to the needs represented in an instructor's class. Either analytic (more detailed, listing several grading criteria) or holistic (more general) rubrics can be used, though some students find analytic rubrics overwhelming and they can be time-consuming for the instructor (Maki, 2010).

While assessment design, grading, and feedback are key areas of concern in any global classroom, assessment in higher education goes beyond these concerns and disciplinary content. It also includes how well students are engaging with global learning and developing a global perspective.

Assessing Global Learning

Assessing global learning begins with considering what we want students to be and/or become regarding their global perspective, often cognitively, intrapersonally, and interpersonally. Since student experiences that contribute to global learning are found in the curriculum, co-curriculum, extra-curriculum, and community, data can be collected from various levels.

Assessing Global Learning at the Institutional Level

Collecting and analyzing data on students' global learning at the institutional level can showcase learning gains, ensure that efforts align, and guide future initiatives. Assessment can occur through purchased inventories or through those that are developed collaboratively in-house. While fee-based inventories offer the benefits of being externally validated and requiring fewer institutional resources in terms of time and staff, their costs can be prohibitive and they can provide data that is less specific to institutional goals. In-house instruments can be less expensive to implement (once development costs are paid off) and can be more focused on institutional priorities; however, creating them can be quite time-intensive and ensuring that key stakeholders are involved in the process can be difficult. Comparing results across groups (minorities, age, gender, grade point average) is often useful for planning and to identify any group(s) that may necessitate special attention. Freely available rubrics can also be modified for an institutional con-text, such as the customization of AAC&U's VALUE Rubrics by Elon University into their Pluralism and Worldview Engagement Rubric or by St. Edward's University into an adapted global learning rubric that is integrated into course-work assignments and assessment (see Nair & Henning, 2017).

Assessment of student learning or perceptions can include Likert-scale surveys, qualitative questions or interviews, or campus-wide focus groups. Students' potential biases or stereotypes or comfort in various situations (e.g., talking with an international peer after class) can be assessed. Including case studies or scenarios helps avoid ambiguity in questions and can lead to a more accurate picture of student learning. Student course evaluations can be aggregated and used as well by adding questions across all coursework and with responses being compared across the institution.

Moving beyond numerical, quantity-driven assessment approaches is necessary in order to spread a cultural commitment to helping students develop a global perspective by faculty, students, and staff. This means moving beyond number of international students or faculty, revenue generation, number of publications co-authored by international researchers, or number of study abroad students. Global learning, as well as its measurement, requires an awareness of how various types of curricula affect the student experience.

The following *Case Study* illustrates various ways that a faculty member in Education assesses global learning, ranging from customizing existing scales or frameworks to creating his own instruments.

CASE STUDY: HOW I ASSESS GLOBAL LEARNING

My approach to assessing global learning stems from my global interdependence philosophy. I believe that the world is a global village of unique diverse communities, and that the diversity of these multiple communities makes it a challenge for individuals to navigate from their community through another community that may, in many cases, be significantly different. Therefore, as citizens of this global village, we should acquire a certain level of global competence in order to function productively and responsibly. I define global competence based on the awareness, knowledge, skills, and attitudes that an individual should continuously develop regarding the world, including its various societies, people, cultures, issues, challenges, and opportunities. I do not believe that individuals are born globally competent. Global competence is acquired through learning. My view of global learning derives from my philosophy of global interdependence of the world and from the concept of global competence. Consequently, I use the constructs of global competence to assess global learning. I have developed two valid and reliable instruments.

The first instrument is the Motivation for Internationalizing Curriculum Scale (MISC), which was developed to assess college and university faculty motivation to internationalize their curriculum (Jean Francois, 2014). This scale can provide information regarding faculty perceptions and attitudes toward global learning. Understanding faculty motivation, attitudes, perceptions, or dispositions to infuse international content into their curriculum is very important for the prospect of students to acquire global competence. The importance resides in the fact that faculty plan, develop, implement, and evaluate the curriculum. The likelihood of students acquiring global competence is strongly related to the willingness of faculty to teach for the development of global competencies.

The second instrument that I developed is called the Cross-Cultural Readiness Exposure Scale (CRES) (Jean Francois, 2015b). The CRES was designed as an instrument to assess the level of readiness of individuals to engage in intercultural interactions or communications. The scale is based on a continuum that spans from ethnocentrism through cultural relativism. The CRES includes sub-scales that assess racism, discrimination, ethnocentrism, prejudice, and stereotype biases, as well as international curiosity, cultural relativism, intercultural communication, and intercultural sensitivity. The CRES helps assess the levels of global awareness of individuals. Results of the CRES can be used to develop training sessions that can help increase the readiness of an individual for intercultural interactions or communications.

In a more micro-context of teaching a course, I use an outcome-based approach to assess global learning. First, I develop specific outcomes based on a given conceptual framework. For example, in some cases, I have used the glocal competence framework to develop specific global learning outcomes (Jean Francois, 2015a). I introduced the glocal competence framework into the literature of global education to emphasize the global competence facets that are rooted in a local context or local reality. In other contexts, I have used the framework of global competence articulated by the Asian Society (https://asiasociety.org/education/what-global-competence) to develop specific global learning outcomes. The global competence constructs of the Asian Society include the ability to investigate the world, recognize perspectives, communicate ideas, and take action. Once I have developed specific global learning outcomes, I set a learning goal related to each outcome and identify learning objectives to achieve each goal. I identify content and activities and finally design assessments (e.g., papers, presentations) to measure whether or not the students have achieved the global learning outcomes. The types of assessments used to measure global learning outcomes vary depending on the conceptual framework used. For example, in the case of a glocal competence framework, assessments measure the awareness, knowledge, skills, and attitudes of students regarding either a) the implications of global issues, challenges, or opportunities for a local community or a given country; or b) the global implications of a local issue, challenge, or opportunity for the world as a global village. In the context of the Asian Society Global Competence

Framework, I might design an assessment to measure the extent to which a student was able to recognize perspectives. In this way, I have worked to operationalize my philosophy into activities and assessments for my students so that we all become more aware of global learning and competence.

Dr. Emmanuel Jean Francois
Associate Professor of Educational Studies
Ohio University

Through this example we can see how faculty can create customized assessments of global learning, from finding useful frameworks or constructs through identifying global learning outcomes to designing assessments based on those outcomes. This process can be followed at the classroom level as well.

Assessing Global Learning at the Curricular and Classroom Level

Curricular planning can be facilitated by periodically assessing work from cohorts for comparison across courses or years. Coursework (e.g., syllabi, assignments) can be analyzed, but student interviews and surveys are options as well. Building an in-house measurement tool implies having clear outputs that can be evaluated (e.g., course materials, faculty e-portfolios, international partnerships).[1] In terms of individual courses, faculty can build or use existing formal and informal assessments to track students' progress in global learning (see Doscher, 2012). These course-based findings can be shared within the department or used only for future course planning. Assessment objectives can include:

- growth over time in specified areas,
- viewing an issue from multiple perspectives,
- comfort with complexity and ambiguity (Musil, 2006),
- holistic thinking about complex issues (Lilley, Barker, & Harris, 2015),
- knowledge about our globalized world, and
- intercultural communication skills.

Faculty may also choose to assess students' level of preparedness for engaging in global experiences (e.g., study abroad, international internships, international service learning), such as with the Cross-Cultural Readiness Exposure Scale (CRES) cited in Emmanuel Jean Francois's *Case Study*.

Data for these assessments can include course evaluations, reflective writing assignments or self-assessments, group project presentations or papers, community-based research projects, simulations, audiovisual recordings of class for later analysis, student presentations (Musil, 2006), e-portfolios, or capstone projects (Lilley et al., 2015). As an example, Pacific Lutheran University built a framework where they created a four-phase global education continuum, outlining the learning objective category (knowledge and intercultural skills, cultural knowledge and skills, global perspectives, and personal commitment) and identified levels and descriptors for each, ranging from introductory to exploratory, participatory, and finally integrative (Musil, 2006). Students in specific courses or internships could then have their work mapped onto this framework, yielding data useful for departmental decision-making. To facilitate planning, faculty can use a global learning course assessment matrix. This begins with the course learning outcomes, moves to assessment methods, then to the evaluation process, minimum criteria for success, a sample, and concludes with assessment results and reflections for improving student learning for future versions of the course. Maintaining a clear relationship between planning at the institutional and classroom levels strengthens the potential for global learning on campus.

The following *Case Study* illustrates how an instructor in the sciences approaches assessment as he works toward his goal of teaching with a global perspective.

CASE STUDY: BRINGING STUDENTS ALONG IN MY JOURNEY TO TEACH WITH A GLOBAL PERSPECTIVE

As an Anatomy & Physiology lab instructor, being able to assess the level of global perspective that my students have at the beginning of the semester is vitally important. This sets the tone for the entire semester of how students approach different challenges, such as communicating effectively with students of a different nationality, understanding the obstacles another student had to overcome to attend college, or being a global citizen ambassador. Gauging where each student is at is rather difficult with over 300 students per semester. Sitting down and having individual conversations with each student is simply impossible.

My solution is to integrate a global perspective assessment into my classroom and lab activities during the first week, and then again at the middle and end of the semester. This allows me to measure these items and gauge students' growth without sacrificing classroom time. I ask my students questions such as, "What is your level of understanding of what it means to be a global citizen?" "On a scale of 1–10 how aware are you of the issues a diverse student (i.e., international, non-majority student) might face in this course?" Or "How willing would you be to reach out to one of these students to learn about their background?"

I use the information I gain to integrate various activities or nuances into class that can help the students develop their global perspective.

As a student myself, I didn't view Anatomy & Physiology as a subject that required much training on being a global citizen. There are foundational Anatomy & Physiology principles that pretty much apply to all human beings. But through the years I realized that believing that all humans think, react, and handle situations the same would be a critical mistake, especially when people interact with other people. That is what makes us human in the first place. This is what makes us different and unique. Regardless of its origin, this factor dictates how students will react to uncomfortable situations, to situations where they are learning new knowledge of someone else, or when being asked to address some deeper issues. Thus, it is essential to assess this factor as soon as I meet new students.

In order to integrate Anatomy & Physiology with this global assessment, I use classroom activities. For example, for one lab assignment I have students determine different anatomical body regions from a packet of pictures provided. In this packet, I've purposefully included many different types of people from various countries, with cultures and appearances. While students are completing this assignment, it allows me to see how students react to questions like, "What do you think of her piercings?" (The picture is of an African woman with large earlobe piercings) and "Have you ever seen that before?" Based upon their answers to questions like those mentioned, I can determine their global perspective level. This also enables me to get to know my students and their background, which is essential for me as an instructor, all while completing an assignment.

For myself, I also have goals. I have a list of questions I ask myself at the beginning of each semester. They include: Have I used globally understood language when describing the lab course expectations? Have I reached out to international students who could be facing a language barrier? Are my teaching assistants aware of the issues they may face this semester as global citizens? Have I created an environment where students can be outstanding global citizens? These questions and the global perspective assessment can be continually asked and integrated into many different labs and situations throughout the semester.

Ian Klein
Lecturer in Biological Sciences
Ohio University

This *Case Study* illustrates how assessment of students' global perspectives can be tailored to course content and also linked to the faculty member's own goals. Faculty can use in-class activities to gather information from students on their perspectives and possible biases or stereotypes which can then guide course planning. Other strategies related to inclusive assessment and assessing global learning follow in the *Classroom Strategies*.

 ## CLASSROOM STRATEGIES

"What strategies can I try in order to fairly assess my students?"

The following strategies can be useful in grading work from diverse students:

- Experiment with ways to structure a course so that the final grade represents student work from throughout the entire term. Including several smaller assessments throughout the term instead of only one or two larger ones can allow students to succeed and build their confidence.
- Build assessments and assignments with feedback in mind. Consider the type of feedback that will likely be most useful for different students (digital, in person, on the paper or exam), and if you will vary that feedback according to student need. Consider which areas students will likely need help with and how they will be able to apply your feedback to future work. Give students access to the rubric you'll use for grading at the same time that you give them the assignment.
- Provide sufficient guidance and clarity in the assessment. Consider having in-class review sessions or providing samples. Students can work in small groups to analyze sample essay questions, identifying strengths and weaknesses as well as possible revisions, or they can collaboratively and constructively critique a sample group presentation for content as well as delivery. Try giving students a substantial list of possible exam questions, telling them the final version will be chosen from the pool. Clarify the role that various language components (e.g., English pronunciation, grammar) will play in the grade.
- Allow student input in the assessment process when possible and create opportunities for students to showcase their strengths. Students can write their own quiz questions (with answers), with the instructor compiling them and administering the quiz to the class.
- Clearly articulate expectations and grading procedures regarding collaboration on projects.

- Consider allowing students to use various reference tools during tests (e.g., bilingual dictionaries), or invite students to submit their assignments early for review, giving them the opportunity to revise before submitting for a grade.
- Give students a menu of options for assignments so they can choose the one(s) most appealing to them, allowing for customization but within stated criteria.

"What are the steps to build a rubric that is fair and customized to my assignments?"

Your rubric will list criteria descriptors down the left column, which can be weighted, and performance descriptors along the top. To create one, consult sources such as Stevens and Levi (2012), and try these steps:

1. Identify the goal of the assessment or activity and what you want from students; reflect on past experiences with grading this assignment and your student population.
2. Identify the learning objectives and criteria descriptors you want to assess. For a rubric for a presentation, the descriptors may be content, preparedness, and presentation skills (volume/posture, eye contact). For a paper, they might be content, organization, and style/mechanics.
3. Next, write the performance descriptors, such as from 1 (excellent) to 3 (unsatisfactory). Reflect on whether any students might feel excluded or unfairly penalized based on these descriptors.
4. Create the layout of your rubric. See online rubric builders for examples or formatting (e.g., iRubric, Quick Rubric, Rubistar).
5. Check that your rubric fits on one page and that the descriptors are comprehensive, concise, clear, and unbiased.
6. Grade sample student work and revise your rubric as needed. Elicit student feedback before using it with the class.

 THE WORKSHOP

8.1 Getting Student Feedback on Course Assessments

It can be difficult to ascertain how students feel about course assessments. It can therefore be useful to gather students' opinions, possibly anonymously.

Write a survey (on paper or online) that asks students what they think the goal or objective of your assessment was, if they think the assessment was fair, and to explain their answers. Concerns might be related to unclear directions or feedback or biases in the assessment. What information did you find from students?

Students' ideas on assessment goal:

Students' feedback about the assessment:

If you have a colleague who teaches a similar course, they can also ask students to answer these questions. How do your answers compare?

Our students agree or disagree about the fairness of the assessment in these ways:

What revisions can you make to your assessments so that students see them as being more fair or inclusive?

Changes I can make based on student feedback:

1.

2.

3.

8.2 Measuring Global Learning in Your Classes

Examine the AAC&U Global Learning VALUE Rubric (www.aacu.org/value/rubrics/global-learning) and the descriptions for each of the levels of proficiency. Choose two or three areas from the six available areas (global self-awareness, perspective taking, cultural diversity, personal and social responsibility, understanding global systems, and applying knowledge to contemporary global contexts). Identify and gather student work that can be evaluated using the rubric. Options include student interviews, papers, presentations, portfolios, self-reports, observations of student behavior, or professor evaluation. Complete the table below for the beginning and ending of the time period you chose, gathering data throughout.

Areas of Global Learning Focus	Student Work	Initial Level	End Level

Areas of Global Learning Focus	Student Work	Initial Level	End Level

Reflect on your students' progress and future opportunities, as well as strategies you may be able to include in the future to help students to develop further. This can be within one course or over several courses. Try looking at some of the resources listed in the bibliography—what information did the assessment help you realize, and what might you vary in your teaching or course planning based on the results you obtained?

 DISCUSSION AND REFLECTION

1. Reflect on the diverse students you have had in class. How might they have felt less prepared for any assessments, even if that was not your intention?
2. Review the four types of formative assessments (declarative learning, procedural learning, conditional learning, and reflective learning). Are you able to use any of these in your classes?
3. Does your institution currently assess global learning? If so, in what ways might the results guide your curriculum or course?
4. Brainstorm three or four questions that would elicit from your students what their level of tolerance is for people with different perspectives. Share your questions and answers with colleagues.
5. Reread the *Case Study*, "Bringing Students Along in my Journey to Teach with a Global Perspective." What goals can you focus on that guide you as you strive to teach with a global perspective? What difficulties do you think your students may face (e.g., with fair assessment, or biases)? How might you help them in these areas?

NOTE

1   See Leask (2015, pp. 124–148) for an example of an extensive reflective faculty questionnaire on the internationalization of the curriculum.

 BIBLIOGRAPHY

AAC&U Sample Quantitative Survey (archive.aacu.org/SharedFutures/documents/Global_ Learning.pdf). Questions in the ten overall sections range from students' reflections on their own thinking to their communication and problem-solving skills.

Astin, W., & Antonio, A. (2012). *Assessment for excellence: The philosophy and practice of assessment and evaluation in higher education* (2nd ed.). Lanham, MD: Rowman & Littlefield.

Beliefs, Events, and Values Inventory (http://thebevi.com/). Mixed-methods analytical tool that helps individuals better understand their beliefs and reflect on how those beliefs and values may facilitate learning.

Boud, D., & Falchikov, N. (2006). Aligning assessment with long-term learning. *Assessment & Evaluation in Higher Education, 31*(4), 399–413.

Critical Thinking Assessment Test from Tennessee Technological University (www.tntech.edu/cat). Assesses skills associated with critical thinking and problem solving, with questions from real world situations and generally requiring short answer essay responses.

Doscher, S. (2012). *The development of rubrics to measure undergraduate students' global awareness and global perspective: A validity study.* FIU Electronic Theses and Dissertations. Paper 588. Retrieved from http://digitalcommons.fiu.edu/etd/588

Driscoll, A., & Wood, S. (2007). *Outcomes-based assessment for learner-centered education.* Sterling, VA: Stylus.

Florida International University's Excellence in Global Learning Medallion honor (http:// fiuonline.fiu.edu/student-experience/development-opportunities/global-medallion/). Award given to students who have "completed an extensive curriculum and co-curriculum designed to enhance global awareness, global perspective, and an attitude of global engagement."

Global Engagement Survey (http://globalsl.org/ges/). Multi-institutional assessment tool composed of seven scales that works to "better understand relationships among program variables and student learning."

Hauck, M., & MacKinnon, T. (2016). A new approach to assessing online intercultural exchange: Soft certification of participant engagement. In R. O'Dowd & T. Lewis (Eds.), *Online intercultural exchange: Policy, pedagogy, practice* (pp. 209–231). New York, NY: Routledge.

Jean Francois, E. (2014). Development of a scale to assess faculty motivation for internationalising their curriculum. *Journal of Further and Higher Education, 38*(5). 641–655.

Jean Francois, E. (2015a). *Building global education with a local perspective: An introduction to glocal higher education.* New York, NY: Palgrave.

Jean Francois, E. (2015b). Development of the cross-cultural readiness exposure scale (CRES). *International Journal of Advanced Multidisciplinary Research and Review*, *3*(5), 10–30.

Lilley, K., Barker, M., & Harris, N. (2015). Educating global citizens: A good 'idea' or an organisational practice? *Higher Education Research & Development*, *34*(5), 957–971.

Maki, P. (2010). *Assessing for learning: Building a sustainable commitment across the institution* (2nd ed.). Sterling, VA: Stylus.

Musil, C. (2006). *Assessing global learning: Matching good intentions with practice*. Association of American Colleges & Universities. Available at: archive.aacu.org/SharedFutures/documents/Global_Learning.pdf

Nair, I., & Henning, M. (2017). *Models of global learning*. Association of American Colleges and Universities. Available at: www.aacu.org/sites/default/files/files/publications/ModelsGlobalLearning.pdf

National Survey of Student Engagement's Global Learning Module (http://nsse.indiana.edu/). Add-on module to main survey and assesses coursework and experiences that emphasize world cultures and issues.

Nilson, L. (2016). *Teaching at its best: A research-based resource for college instructors* (4th ed.). San Francisco, CA: Jossey-Bass.

Pluralism and Worldview Engagement Rubric (www.ifyc.org/sites/default/files/u4/PluralismWorldviewEngagementRubric2.pdf). Created and customized by Elon University based on AAC&U's VALUE Rubrics.

Ryan, J. (2005). Improving teaching and learning practices for international students: Implications for curriculum, pedagogy, and assessment. In J. Carroll & J. Ryan (Eds.), *Teaching international students: Improving learning for all* (pp. 92–100). London, UK: Routledge.

Stevens, D., & Levi, A. (2012). *Introduction to rubrics: An assessment tool to save grading time, convey effective feedback, and promote student learning* (2nd ed.). Sterling, VA: Stylus.

Suskie, L. (2018). *Assessing student learning: A common sense guide* (3rd ed.). San Francisco, CA: Jossey-Bass.

University of Waterloo Centre for Teaching Excellence (https://uwaterloo.ca/centre-for-teaching-excellence/teaching-resources/teaching-tips/tips-students/self-directed-learning/self-directed-learning-learning-contracts). Detailed instructions and examples of learning contracts.

Walvoord, B. (2010). *Assessment clear and simple: A practical guide for institutions, departments and general education*. San Francisco, CA: Jossey-Bass.

Waterfield, J., & West, B. (2010). *Inclusive assessment: Diversity and inclusion, the assessment challenge*. University of Bradford. Available at: www.pass.brad.ac.uk/wp5inclusion.pdf

Conclusion

Not long ago, the concepts of "global citizenship" and "teaching with a global perspective" were goals that seemed more aspirational than feasible in higher education. With increasing campus commitments and models to follow, however, it is now apparent that we can all find pathways to building environments where students and faculty choose to embrace a global perspective. Campuses that are succeeding in global education are those that have expanded beyond focusing almost exclusively on the teaching of content knowledge about the world (e.g., geography, politics, religions) and now add to that real-world experiences for students to build the attitudes of respect, empathy and the intercultural skills necessary for a global perspective to develop. Teaching with a global perspective involves noticing the struggles facing our student populations, such as those outlined in Chapter 1, and identifying opportunities to help them integrate into and succeed on our campuses.

Global citizenship is thus an ongoing process. As educators, we can model empathy and intercultural communication and an awareness that we also have much to learn as we seek to become more adept in meeting the needs of our diverse students. Many of the case studies in this book (such as that of Winsome Chunnu in Chapter 2) outline the importance of authentic relationships and modeling lifelong learning in working with students as they begin their own journey into global citizenship. This relationship-based approach can be operationalized in our teaching in other ways as well. The faculty we've worked with have made the simple but powerful choice to look at their own classes and the sub-groups represented, for example by bringing in guest speakers or asking students to do "Spotlight Presentations" featuring various cultures and backgrounds represented in their department. Another professor revised course learning outcomes to include global learning and then added a reflective, low-stakes writing activity that allows her to get to know and develop relationships with all of her students instead of only the most vocal. We can seek to give students space in our classrooms where they can draw on their own experiences and relate them to peers and class content.

Teaching with a global perspective also entails becoming more comfortable with leading classes of diverse students and helping them learn from each other. Technology now allows us to bring students together to learn from new or different groups of people, such as the online intercultural exchange described by Sheida Shirvani (Chapter 2), or with a professor who now incorporates a small collaborative assignment that asks students to meet new students, or one who expanded her First Day Student Survey to leverage the power of diversity when forming study groups. Purba Das's activity asking students to analyze their own identities (Chapter 3) helps them realize that how they view others is just a fraction of who that person is. There are many ways to nudge students beyond their initial biases; we can also help them recognize their own hidden diversity and how that impacts their views of others and, thus, communication. These faculty have all found and embraced the diversity in their classes yet also led students toward identifying the experiences and realities they do share.

Providing diverse populations of students with the support they need is crucial to teaching with a global perspective. Students may need support as they develop their intercultural communication skills—working through miscommunications, understanding others' accents, becoming a thoughtful listener, or engaging with a peer different from themselves. Mick Andzulis's example (Chapter 4) illustrates his course revisions to elicit more participation and build in more scaffolding as he challenged students to provide each other with more meaningful feedback; his decision to encourage students to not only collaborate with someone from a different background, but also even conduct interviews in a language other than English demonstrates the creativity and open borders that we can bring to our courses. Linda Trautman's course-long series of tasks (Chapter 5) to help students trust each other and be willing to listen to other perspectives gives us hope and reminds us of the power in planning and human interactions.

Institution-wide initiatives play a major role in moving a university forward in global education (see Edmonds and Jang in Chapter 2), but equally important are the efforts made by individual departments, faculty, and staff. In Chapter 8, when Ian Klein and Emmanuel Jean Francois share how they approach the assessment of global learning, we can see pathways to articulating these concepts to our students. In Chapter 7 we see stories of students like Amanda Hayes who have found voices that reflect their heritages and expectations. In Chapter 6, we see examples of students who have found their identities in the midst of larger departmental or university concerns. For many faculty, the first steps in prioritizing global learning are including a global perspective in their course learning objectives and openly discussing these goals with their students.

Through this book, we suggest that higher education move toward a comprehensive model of inclusion, recognizing the range of diversities in our classrooms and identifying strategies that allow for the success of all types of students not only academically, but also as they develop as global citizens. As one faculty learning community participant commented, "I want all of my students to feel included and valued. I also want them to recognize that we are all global citizens, who benefit from connecting with people who are dissimilar from us." We couldn't agree more.

Index

Note: Figures are indicated in *italics* and tables in **bold**.